Savior

40 Days
with the
Savior

PREPARING YOUR
HEART FOR
EASTER

—❧—

HENRY GARIEPY

THOMAS NELSON PUBLISHERS
Nashville • Atlanta • London • Vancouver

Published in Nashville, Tennessee, by Thomas Nelson, Inc., Publishers, and
distributed in Canada by Word Communications, Ltd., Richmond, British
Columbia, and in the United Kingdom by Word (UK), Ltd., Milton Keynes,
England.

Unless otherwise noted, Scripture quotations are from the NEW KING JAMES
VERSION. Copyright © 1979, 1980, 1982, Thomas Nelson, Inc., Publishers.

Scripture quotations noted KJV are from the The Holy Bible, KING JAMES
VERSION.

Scripture quotations noted NIV are taken from the HOLY BIBLE, NEW
INTERNATIONAL VERSION®. Copyright © 1973, 1978, 1984 by
International Bible Society. Used by permission of Zondervan Bible Publishing
House. All rights reserved.

The "NIV" and "New International Version" trademarks are registered in the
United States Patent and Trademark Office by International Bible Society. Use
of either trademark requires the permission of International Bible Society.

Scripture quotations noted PHILLIPS are from J.B. PHILLIPS: THE NEW
TESTAMENT IN MODERN ENGLISH, Revised Edition. Copyright © J.B.
Phillips 1958, 1960, 1972. Used by permission of Macmillan Publishing Co.,
Inc.

Library of Congress Cataloging-in-Publication Data

Gariepy, Henry
    40 Days with the Savior : preparing your heart for Easter / Henry
Gariepy.
      p.   cm.
    ISBN 0-7852-8005-7 (pbk.)
    1. Jesus Christ—Passion—Meditations.   2. Lent—Prayers-books and
devotions.   3. Devotional calendars.
I. title.   II. Title: Forty days with the Savior.
BT431.G37 1995
232.96—dc20   94-31419
                                            CIP

Printed in the United States of America
1 2 3 4 5 6 7 — 01 00 99 98 97 96 95

To Priscilla Radtke
Sister in the Lord
and lifelong encourager in my ministry

CONTENTS

INTRODUCTION

The tiny hill of Calvary has become the pinnacle of history which towers over all other events. The world has gloried in its cross—carved it into every form of beauty, emblazoned it on the flags of nations, and engraved it on the scepters and diadems of kings. The mighty impact of Calvary divided time in two. Christ's death made Calvary the door through which humanity might enter eternity.

"The cross transforms everything," writes John R. W. Stott in his seminal book *The Cross of Christ* (Downers Grove: InterVarsity Press, 1986). He states, "The cross lies at the center of the historic, biblical faith." Indeed, the word *cross* comes from the Latin *crux* which means the essential or deciding point. The cross is the central point of history. The destiny of every soul lies in the promise of the cross.

No theme is so sacred, so sublime, as the suffering and death of Christ on Calvary. It was on the cross that the Son of God paid the tremendous cost for our salvation and eternal life. It was on the cross that Christ balanced mankind's ledger with God, wiping out our spiritual bankruptcy before a holy and just God.

These forty meditations may serve as a pilgrimage of the soul, journeying through the final week and sufferings in the life of our Lord. They will help us reverently contemplate the sublime sacrifice of our Lord and draw us nearer to the cross and its mighty meaning for our lives.

Why forty meditations? The number forty has sacred significance in Scripture and Christian history. When the hope of the world was sheltered in the Ark, there was rain upon the earth for forty days (Gen. 7:17). Israel's wilderness wanderings lasted for forty years, during which God provided manna for their sustenance (Ex. 16:35; Num. 32:13). Moses tarried on Mount Sinai for forty days when God gave the Ten Commandments (Ex. 24:18). Israel's spies scouted the Promised Land for forty days (Num. 13:1–25). Elijah tarried in Horeb forty days before God's revelation to him (1 Kings 19:8). Jesus fasted in the wilderness for forty days after which He overcame the tempting of the devil (Luke 4:2). Our Lord remained after His resurrection, confirming the faith of His followers in that critical period, for forty days (Acts 1:3).

Christians traditionally commemorate the forty days before Easter as Lent, remembering the suffering and sacrifice of Christ. It is a time devoted to meditation, self-examination, discipline, and renewal. Ash Wednesday inaugurates Lent with prayer and Holy Week before Easter. Good Friday is Lent's climax.

These forty meditations can serve as devotional readings during the Lenten period or for any season when one is led to contemplate the sacred last week of the life of our Lord and its meaning for us. When we come to the end of these reflections, let us affirm with the Apostle Paul, "God forbid that I should boast except in the cross of our Lord Jesus Christ" (Gal. 6:14).

Men and women throughout history have discovered the great hope of the cross. Aleksandr Solzhenitsyn for many years was a prisoner in Soviet concentration camps. His days were made up of backbreaking labor and slow starvation. One day he gave up, feeling no purpose in fighting on. Laying his shovel down, he walked over to a bench and sat down. He knew that the penalty for sitting down was death. At any moment a guard might order him to get up, and when he failed to respond, the guard would probably beat him to death with a shovel. Solzhenitsyn had seen it happen many times.

As he was sitting there waiting for death, he felt a presence near. He lifted his eyes and saw an old man with a wrinkled, utterly expressionless face. They had never communicated because prisoners were not allowed to talk. This old man took a stick, and in the sand at Solzhenitsyn's feet he drew the sign of the cross. As Solzhenitsyn stared at that cross his entire perspective shifted. He realized in that moment that the cross was the hope of mankind, even against the all-powerful Soviet Empire. He slowly got up, picked up the shovel, and went back to work under the power of the cross, later to become a prophetic voice to the nations.

The cost of Christian discipleship has always been the same. Christ still calls: "If anyone desires to come after Me, let him deny himself, and take up his cross, and follow Me" (Matt. 16:24). Our Lord still summons us to walk the pathway of the cross.

Love's arms were never stretched so wide as upon the cross. May the chorus of "Lead Me to Calvary" be our prayer as we commence our pilgrimage to Calvary:

> Lest I forget Gethsemane,
> Lest I forget thine agony,
> Lest I forget thy love to me,
> Lead me to Calvary.

I
Pilgrimage To Calvary

*Looking unto Jesus, the author and finisher of
our faith, who for the joy that was set before
him endured the cross.—Heb. 12:2*

A man standing on the deck of a ship suddenly
heard a deafening rumble as a volcano on the shore
burst into flame. The whole countryside was lit up,
and then the flame died. In those moments, he
said, was revealed the fire that is ever burning in
the heart of that mountain.

As we contemplate the Passion of our Lord, His
suffering on Calvary, we have a glimpse of the love
that is forever in the heart of God for each of us.
Calvary is the supreme articulation of God's love
for the world. As we ponder the stupendous scene
of the Son of God impaled on a felon's cross on
our behalf, we are constrained with Charles Wesley
to exclaim:

Amazing love! how can it be
That Thou, my God, shouldst die for me?

Our pilgrimage to Calvary ushers us into the Holy of Holies in the sanctuary of Christ's life. We stand before one of the most sublime and sacred truths of eternity. Spiritually speaking, we should "take off our shoes," for we are on holy ground. Members of the Roman Catholic Church have a form of worship termed "Stations of the Cross." For the Catholic worship it is an experience of devotional meditation in remembrance of Christ's journey from the house of Pilate to Calvary. This act of worship dates back to around 1350 and consists of fourteen meditations before crosses and pictures depicting the sufferings of Christ. The Stations are depicted on the walls of the church and the worshiper pauses, reflects, and prays at each one.

Protestant churches do not have such a rite for remembering the Passion of Christ. But we may be faithful in calling to mind the sorrow and suffering of our Lord on our behalf. This study can perhaps serve as our "Stations of the Cross," giving opportunity to pause and pray as we ponder the amazing love so powerfully expressed on Calvary.

The writer of Hebrews invokes just such a contemplation: "Looking unto Jesus, the author and finisher of our faith, who for the joy that was set before Him endured the cross, despising the shame, and has sat down at the right hand of the throne of God" (Heb. 12:2). May our contemplation lead to a deeper consecration of ourselves to the One whose love surpasses our understanding but wins our hearts.

—ᕕ—

Dear Savior, lest I forget Your love to me, lead me in Your path of suffering all the way to the foot of the cross.

2
Man of Sorrows

He is . . . a Man of sorrows.—Isa. 53:3

Centuries before Jesus came to earth the prophet Isaiah declared that He would be "a Man of sorrows."

Man of Sorrows. This is one of the cardinal titles of Christ. Some notable men are men of wealth, some are men of fame, some are men of pleasure, but Christ was a man of sorrows. He was the Prince of martyrs, the Lord of anguish, the King of suffering. Some of His closest followers might forsake Him, but His sorrows were always with Him.

The last week of Christ's earthly life, with its record of deep sorrow, looms predominantly in the Gospels. One-third of Matthew, one-third of Mark, one-fourth of Luke, and one-half of John's Gospel are devoted to the last week of the life of Jesus.

This is a striking contrast to the few pages of biography covering the death of other men of history. An example is a biography of Abraham Lincoln with only twenty-five out of its five thousand pages relating the dramatic account of the assassination and death. The amount of space in the Gospels devoted to Christ's suffering and death is so disproportionate that it underscores the paramount value of that period in His life and ministry.

In contrast, two of the Gospels do not have anything to say about the birth of Christ. Two give no record of the temptation, two offer no record of the Sermon on the Mount, two give no account of the Ascension, and one of the Gospels includes none of Jesus' incomparable parables. But each Gospel writer gives extensive detail and coverage to the suffering and death of Christ.

Philip Bliss was inspired by Isaiah's description of Christ to write his enduring hymn:

> Man of sorrows! what a name
> For the Son of God, Who came
> Ruined sinners to reclaim;
> Hallelujah! What a Savior!
>
> Bearing shame and scoffing rude,
> In my place condemned He stood,
> Sealed my pardon with His blood;
> Hallelujah! What a Savior!
>
> Lifted up was He to die;
> "It is finished!" was His cry;
> Now in heaven, exalted high;
> Hallelujah! What a Savior!

Man of Sorrows, I begin walking the path-
way of Your suffering with awe and adora-
tion that You should endure such suffering
on my behalf.

3
The Wounded Healer

He was wounded for our transgressions.—
Isa. 53:5

Some years ago, when we were having family devotions, one of our little girls was struck by the fact that Jesus had to endure the suffering and agony of Calvary. Unaware of the depth of her question, she asked in deep sincerity, "But if Jesus was God, why did He have to die?"

As we contemplate the unmatched sorrows and suffering of Christ, we cannot help but ask why. Isaiah answers this question for us with immortal words:

Surely He has borne our griefs
    And carried our sorrows . . .
But He was wounded for our transgressions,
    He was bruised for our iniquities;
The chastisement for our peace was upon Him,
    And by His stripes we are healed.
All we like sheep have gone astray;
    We have turned, every one, to his own way;

And the LORD has laid on Him
the iniquity of us all. (53:4–6)

As we contemplate the sufferings of our Lord,
let us remember the great purpose of His Passion.
Isaiah again reminds us, "For the transgressions of
My people He was stricken. . . . And He bore
the sin of many, and made intercession for the
transgressors" (53:8,12).

At the Fall the deadly venom of sin entered the
bloodstream of humanity. A holy God could not
tolerate sin in His universe. Humankind was under
the condemnation of sin. We were helpless and
hopeless. But God in His infinite love provided
the only way of salvation. Christ came to earth,
lived, suffered, and died, and on the cross made
the scarlet payment for our sin that we might be
redeemed and have life eternal.

Cecil Alexander's hymn, in beautiful simplicity,
extols this sublime truth:

There is a green hill far away,
    Without a city wall,
Where the dear Lord was crucified
    Who died to save us all.

We may not know, we cannot tell
    What pains He had to bear;
But we believe it was for us
    He hung and suffered there.

He died that we might be forgiven,
  He died to make us good,
That we might go at last to Heaven,
  Saved by His precious blood.

There was no other good enough
  To pay the price of sin
He only could unlock the gate
  Of Heaven, and let us in.

—◊—

*Dear Savior, I am eternally in debt for
Your wounding that brings my healing and
Your dying that brings my salvation.*

4
The
Upper Room

*"He will show you a large, furnished upper
room; there make ready."*—Luke 22:12

Jesus' meeting with His disciples in the Upper
Room signals the beginning of our Lord's Passion.
There He met for the final time with His intimate
friends in the sadness of farewell.

Luke describes the intriguing and special preparation by our Lord for the Last Supper. When Jesus
told Peter and John to go and make preparation
they asked, "'Where do you want us to prepare?'
And He said to them, 'Behold, when you have
entered the city, a man will meet you carrying a
pitcher of water; follow him into the house which
he enters. Then you shall say to the master of the
house, "The Teacher says to you, 'Where is the
guest room where I may eat the Passover with My
disciples?'" Then he will show you a large, furnished upper room; there make ready.' So they went
and found it just as He had said to them, and they
prepared the Passover" (22:9–13).

Our Lord's special selection and preparation denotes the sacredness He attached to that Upper Room experience with His disciples. In the Upper Room, "He was troubled in spirit" (John 13:21), as He announced that one of their company would betray Him. It was there that Satan entered into the heart of Judas in the first act of his foul plot (John 13:27). It was there Jesus predicted Peter's denial of Him (John 13:38). It was there Jesus announced that the hour of His Passion had come: "Indeed the hour is coming, yes, has now come, that you will be scattered" (John 16:32).

And it was in the Upper Room that our Lord entered into intimate fellowship with His disciples. It was there He spoke the immortal words that have resonated across the centuries to His followers of every age.

An "Upper Room experience" in our day is a time of blessing and fellowship with the Lord. We cannot roll back the centuries and enter into the divine communion of that Upper Room as did those first disciples. But we can know the close fellowship and the presence of our Lord. We too can hear His word and precious promises to us. We too can affirm our love and loyalty to Him. And from that Upper Room we can follow His footsteps to the cross, and on to His mighty triumph in our world today.

As did the disciples of old, we must come to the cross by way of the Upper Room. To understand

Calvary we need to know His presence, listen to His Word, and obey His commands.

———◆◆◆———

Dear Lord, as I trace Your footsteps to Calvary, lead me to an Upper Room experience of divine communion and consecration.

5

The Place of the Upper Room

And when they had entered, they went up into
the upper room.—Acts 1:13

The Upper Room where Jesus met for the Last Supper with His disciples is believed to have been in the home of John Mark. It is worthy of note that this most intimate communion among Jesus and His followers took place in the common setting of a home. And later, it was the same upper room that hosted the great outpouring of the Holy Spirit at Pentecost. There God bestowed His highest gift to humankind, the gift of Himself.

God still draws near to us in the ordinary, commonplace, everyday experience and places. To the heart that is attuned to Him, He comes in surprising ways and places. We may encounter in the most unexpected moments and places the One who said, "Watch, be ready, for in an hour that you think not the Son of man comes." C. S. Lewis has stated that the incursion of the miraculous is "as intimate as breathing."

Watch out Moses, that bush aflame in the backside of the desert is the Lord! Peter, look up, the Lord of the universe is standing there, right on the pebbled shore of your lake! Woman of Samaria, imagine meeting the Messiah right there by the well to which you come each day! And Matthew, as you endure the dull routine of writing tax receipts, do you ever dream of meeting the One who will inspire you to write the greatest story ever told? Cleopas, see how He floods that prosaic country road with His peerless glory? And Simon of Cyrene, of all places, to meet God—carrying a cross to a felon's death! Indeed, our Lord is all about us!

He is apt to reveal Himself to us in any place, at any time, in any fashion. As Helmut Thielicke has stated it, "We live by God's surprises!" The Lord is no respecter of persons and He is no respecter of places. The One who shared His most intimate communion in the common setting of a home loves to come to us in our common places and experiences of life.

Religion so often seems to be afflicted with spiritual compartmentalization. We tend to divide our lives into compartments and to think we can experience God's presence only through certain structured rituals and in certain places. We are prone to restrict our religious expressions and experience to certain places, times, and rituals.

The Upper Room eloquently proclaims that He is the Lord of the commonplace as well as the unusual. We may find the warmth and beauty of

His presence and hear His gracious word to us just where we are!

———∞———

Lord of the universe, who came in intimate fellowship in the humble setting of a home, come to my life in its ordinariness. Set aglow its commonplace with the radiance of Your presence.

6

The Presence in the Upper Room

"Yet I am among you as the One who serves.
. . . And I bestow upon you a kingdom."
—Luke 22:27, 29

The presence of Christ is the central focus of
the Upper Room. It was the presence of our Lord
that transformed that humble room into a Holy of
Holies. Here was the Sovereign who had come to
be our Savior. The infinite had become the intimate to that company of disciples. The very Lord
of the universe there imparted eternal truths to
His followers. The God of unspeakable love announced in that room that He came as One who
serves and that He would soon confer to them an
eternal kingdom.

The presence of Christ in the Upper Room has
often been highlighted by artists. Usually they
have silhouetted Him against a window or in some
other way made Him the center of attention, the
dominant presence. For indeed it is His presence
that immediately captivates our attention as we
cross the threshold of that room.

I asked Dr. Scott Peck, author of the best-selling

book *The Road Less Traveled*, what sort of relationship he had with Jesus Christ when he was writing his book. He shared how he read the Gospels to research the life of Christ, and then he said with a strong conviction: "I was absolutely thunderstruck by the man I found in the Gospels. I encountered this extraordinary real human being, and I found myself beginning to fall in love with Jesus." To perceive who Jesus really is should have a profound and transforming effect upon us, just as it did for Scott Peck.

Those with Christ in that hour of final fellowship would never be able to forget the impact of His presence in that room. His words to them that night were indelibly inscribed upon their hearts and recorded for His followers through the ages. Indeed, those with Him on that night of nights were a motley crowd, but they were the raw material from which Christ began to build His kingdom. Forget the pictures we have seen of venerable disciples with flowing white hair and beards. They were young men—red-blooded, high-spirited doers and dreamers who, because they were with Him, were destined to turn the world upside down.

There was John the mystic, Thomas who always looked before he leaped, Peter who always leaped before he looked, Matthew with his gift of penmanship and detail, Andrew with his warm friendliness, and the others. We may well see mirrored somewhere in that company a reflection of ourselves—our own weakness and deep needs, our own aspirations and potential for the kingdom.

The central presence in the Upper Room is the One of whom Charles Wesley petitioned:

> Love divine, all loves excelling,
> Joy of heaven to earth come down.
> Fix in us Thy humble dwelling,
> All Thy faithful mercies crown.
> Jesus, Thou art all compassion,
> Pure, unbounded love Thou art;
> Visit us with Thy salvation,
> Enter every trembling heart.

Christ, whose presence was central in that Upper Room, be the center and focus in all of my life.

7

The Passover in the Upper Room

"Go and prepare the Passover for us,
that we may eat."—Luke 22:8

Jesus met with His disciples in that final hour for the sacred and solemn observance of the Passover supper.

Together they drank from the cup of the Kiddush, the cup of sanctification, a rite which distinguished this meal from common meals. The head of the supper prayed over the cup, and then drank its wine.

The solemn feast included hand washings, breaking of bread, recounting the story of Israel's deliverance, the grace, the meal, prayer of thanksgiving, and the psalms. Ritual and symbolism underscored a people's worship and gratitude to God.

The disciples, following Jesus' command, prepared the lamb that was to remind them of Israel having been saved by the blood of the lamb when they were in Egypt. The disciples also prepared unleavened bread such as their ancestors ate in haste when they escaped from slavery, a bowl of salt water to remind them of the tears shed and the waters of the Red Sea, a collection of bitter herbs to remind them of the bitterness of slavery, a paste to remember the clay of which they had made brick during their slavery, and four cups of wine to be drunk at different stages of the meal. For the Jew, the Passover Feast was much more than a ritual; it was a commemoration of the power and mercy of God.

At the end of the supper there was the Eucharist or thanksgiving. Over this memorial meal with all its sacred significance, we read, "He . . . gave thanks" (Luke 22:17). A startling fact! Death was just outside the door, yet Jesus gave thanks.

For seven days following Passover, the Jews observed the Feast of Unleavened Bread. The Jewish family diligently searched the house by the light of a candle to be sure no leaven was in the house. If leaven were found in the house, the people of the household would be cut off from the nation in their spiritual heritage.

There are rich insights and sacred applications for us to glean from our Lord's Passover supper in the Upper Room. We too must remember and celebrate the Lord's mighty deliverance of our life from the oppression and bondage of sin. We too should remember to give thanks for His grace. Those of us who have made our spiritual exodus out of "Egypt's bondage," who have been delivered by Christ, need to search out every dark corner of the heart to purge any malignant leaven of sin and self.

———❦———

Lord, as I contemplate the scene in that Upper Room, lead me to deeper devotion by a faithful remembrance of all You have done for me.

8

The
Passover Lamb

*For indeed Christ, our Passover, was sacrificed
for us.—1 Cor. 5:7*

The Passover lamb, specially prepared, provided the meal at the Last Supper in the Upper Room. The Passover lamb symbolizes the atoning sacrifice of Christ.

According to the historian Josephus, a census during the reign of Nero revealed that 256,500 lambs were slain at the Passover time. The law required that there must be a minimum of ten people to one lamb. Every adult male Jew who lived within 15 miles of Jerusalem was required to celebrate the Passover there. Others came to Jerusalem from around the world.

But on the night that Jesus and His disciples shared the Last Supper, a new and greater Passover Lamb had come. The deliverance by this perfect paschal lamb was to be far more extensive and efficacious. Now the Son of God was to become the Passover Lamb for all men of all time. No longer would the lamb need die. Christians could then gladly exclaim, "Christ, our Passover, was sacrificed for us" (1 Cor. 5:7).

Christ fulfilled the allegory as our Passover Lamb. The Passover lamb had to be a "lamb from the flock." Christ was God come to the community of mankind. He became one of the "flock" of humanity.

It was required that the lamb be without blemish. This qualification excluded blind, broken, bruised, maimed, ulcerous, scurvied, scabbed, crushed, and castrated lambs. No defects were allowed. So Christ was without stain, without spot—altogether pure and perfect. The Passover lamb had to be in the prime of its life, a "male of the first year." Jesus was cut off in the prime of His life. Not a bone of the Passover lamb could be broken. Although it was customary for soldiers to break the knees of men dying on the cross, Jesus' bones were not broken. Thus, the requirements of the Passover lamb were kept and prophecy was fulfilled.

The Passover lamb was slain at evening. The very hour that Jesus hung on the cross is believed to have been the time the Passover lamb was slaughtered for this memorial feast.

Those who applied the blood of the lamb to the doorposts were delivered from death in Egypt's land. Our Passover Lamb spares from eternal death those whose lives have had applied the blood that flowed from Calvary's cross. In His blood alone is our deliverance from sin's bondage and death.

—∞—

Christ, our Passover Lamb, I praise and thank You that by Your loving and perfect sacrifice I am redeemed.

9
The Paradox of the Upper Room

He poured water into a basin and began to
wash the disciples' feet.—John 13:5

It was a sight that evoked awe and adoration. The Lord of the universe girded Himself with a towel, took a basin of water, and performed the duty of a slave. He washed the feet of those who, apart from their quarrelsomeness, should have bathed His.

We cannot begin to grasp the divine humility involved in this simple act of service—the Highest stooping to the lowest, the Sovereign becoming the servant, the Son of God assuming the role of the slave of men.

Peter saw this act of Jesus as unthinkable and cried out, "Lord, are You going to wash my feet? . . . No, You shall never wash my feet." Jesus replied, "Unless I wash you, you have no part with Me." Peter responds, "Then, Lord, not just my feet but my hands and my head as well!"

Our Lord then gives the meaning of His symbolic act: "You call Me Teacher and Lord, and you say well, for so I am. If I then, your Lord and Teacher, have washed your feet, you also ought to wash one another's feet. For I have given you an example, that you should do as I have done to you" (John 13:13–15). Here in the Upper Room the Lord of creation gives to humankind the greatest lesson of the ages on humility and servanthood.

The sight of this paradox in the Upper Room staggers the imagination, but it captures the heart. It demonstrates to what depths the Son of God was willing to go to meet our need. This example of, in Bonhoeffer's pregnant phrase, the "sublime otherism," is for each of us a mandate for the servant role to which we are called. Christ by this peerless example of humility reminds us that those who would qualify as saints must validate their credentials as servants.

When astronaut James Irwin returned from his walk on the moon, he realized many would now think of him as a celebrity. But humbled by the glory of God he had seen on his mission and by the goodness of God in his life, he testified: "As I was returning to earth, I realized that I was not a celebrity, but a servant. I am here as God's servant on planet Earth to share what I have experienced that others might know the glory of God." His words may serve as a good motto for all of us— "Not a celebrity, but a servant."

"For even the Son of Man did not come to be served, but to serve, and to give His life a ransom for many" (Mark 10:45). As with Peter, who saw his need for a washing of more than the dust of the road from his feet, so may we pray for a total cleansing to be worthy servants of our Lord. In the words of Albert Orsborn's song, may we pray:

Wash from my hands the dust of earthly striving;
    Take from my mind the stress of secret fear;
Cleanse Thou the wounds from all but Thee far
      hidden,
    And when the waters flow let my healing
      appear.

Light, life and love are in that healing fountain,
    All I require to cleanse me and restore;
Flow through my soul, redeem its desert places,
    And make a garden there for the Lord I adore.

—m—

Lord, cleanse my feet to follow You, my hands to serve You, my mind to know You, and my heart to love You.

10

The Preachment in the Upper Room

"Let not your heart be troubled; you believe in God."—John 14:1

Last words are often weighted with great importance. We hang on to the last words of those near and dear to us as they share that which is deepest on their hearts. The last words of Jesus to His followers before His death are those He spoke in the Upper Room.

Our Lord's farewell discourse within those walls is His longest recorded discourse in Scripture, comprising five chapters in the Gospel of John (13—17). This sublime meditation is the last will and testament of Jesus Christ to His followers.

The immortal words of our Master, floating like soft music through the night air, resonate with timeless truths across the centuries. Here we find the eleventh commandment of love, the incomparable "Let not your heart be troubled," the instructive parable of the vine, the vital teaching on the Holy Spirit.

The words spoken in the dim light of that room

represent the most important truths Jesus had to share with His disciples. He selected this hour to impart to them that which they needed most to know. This night loomed as the supreme hour of test and trial for the company gathered there. For our Lord, the shadow of the cross now fell across that room. For the disciples, in a matter of hours they would be scattered. Their world would come crashing in chaos about them. More than any other moment Jesus needed to tell them to hold on, to trust, to "believe in God" and "believe in Me."

The moment of supreme testing comes to every life. A tragedy overtakes us. Our faith is beset by a great trial and testing. Some storm of life in all its savage fury beats upon us. At that moment only the deep truths of eternity will sustain us. Christ imparts more than a creed; He gives Himself, declaring, "I am the way, the truth, and the life" (John 14:6).

As our Lord is about to take leave of His followers, He flings out His peerless promise, "I will come again" (John 14:3). The return of Christ is the cornerstone upon which the kingdom of God is founded. It is the culmination of all prophecy, the motivation for evangelism, and the blessed hope of every believer.

How vital it would be for the disciples then, and for future believers, to know that the cross would not be the end. There would be a bright tomorrow. There is a glorious hope.

In Christ's preachment in the Upper Room, we have the essential truths of the gospel. We learn that His suffering and death purchased our salvation and life eternal, that He will return in mighty triumph, and that the Holy Spirit will come to His followers to guide, empower, and indwell.

—————

Divine Teacher, may Your immortal words be grafted on my heart so I will better know and do Your will.

11
The Peace of the Upper Room

"Peace I leave with you, My peace I give to you."—John 14:27

As we continue with Christ in the Upper Room we are surprised to hear fall from His lips the word *peace*.

Peace in the midst of tragedy? Peace in the midst of great sorrow? Peace in the midst of death? Peace when their futures were blackest?

Peace? When just outside the door of that Upper Room awaited the betrayals and shadows of Gethsemane, the travesty of the trials, the violence and ignominy of Calvary?

But peace is the word Christ spoke in the Upper Room as He confidently said to His disciples: "Peace I leave with you, My peace I give to you. . . . Let not your heart be troubled, neither let it be afraid." In that moment, not panic, but peace prevailed.

Now, there is a peace which is easy to understand. It is the peace that prevails when no clouds are in sight, when we feel neither pain nor sorrow, when the road of life is smooth and without real danger. But those were not the circumstances of the Upper Room. Jesus spoke of His peace in quite a different setting. All the ingredients for despair were within those walls. Outside that Upper Room, the air of the city was electric with the storm about to burst upon Him in all its fury. He could feel something of the excruciating pain and anguish that is just outside those doors. Treason had entered into the heart of one of His most trusted friends. Desertion and death were imminent. This is the setting in which Jesus bequeathed to the disciples His peace.

Who is it that dares to utter the word *peace* amid history's greatest tragedy? The word is spoken with the authority of the Sovereign of the world, the One who is to become the mighty conqueror over death and the grave. He who triumphed over life's greatest tragedy is the One who speaks peace and who bestows it to His followers.

And what is the word of Christ today to our troubled and tortured world? What has He to say to a world haunted with deep fears? To a world beset with terrorism, strife, wars, famine, turmoil? What word does He speak to a generation that lives under the shadow of nuclear holocaust?

Is not His word still true for us today? Does He not still come in the midst of our fears and failures, our sorrows and sufferings, and speak His assuring promise, "My peace I give to you."

For true peace is not a matter of circumstance. Peace does not come with possessions, or power, or pleasures. Nor does it come with security in our world of terror and violence. True peace is found only in Jesus Christ. It is His gift to us when through His Spirit, He lives within us. He alone stills our restlessness and bestows inner calm amid life's outer storm.

Peace is the legacy of Christ to His followers: "Peace I leave with you; My peace I give to you." As He did with His first disciples, He wants to give us His gift of peace. He wants to transform our troubles into trust, our problems into promises, our fears into faith. Let us appropriate His rich gift to our heart and life.

—⚇—

Prince of Peace, grant to me Your precious gift of peace.

12
The Power in the Upper Room

"The Helper . . . I will send Him to you."
—John 16:7

As long as Jesus was with His disciples, they had the guidance and reinforcement of His presence. But now He would be gone. Days of persecution and severe testings were ahead. Their great need was for something that somehow could take the place of Christ. No one on earth was equal to that. They would need power. Superhuman power.

As we linger with the Lord in the Upper Room, we hear Him impart His greatest legacy to His followers—the gift of the Holy Spirit: "And I will pray the Father, and He will give you another Helper, that He may abide with you forever—the Spirit of truth" (John 14:16–17). It is the highest gift of God to the believer—the gift of the Giver, none other than God Himself, to dwell within the Christian.

The Greek word here for the Spirit is *parakletos*. It is derived from two words: *para* (beside) and *kaleo* (call), denoting one who is called beside us. The

Holy Spirit is the One who is with us to guide, cleanse, produce holy living, and give us power to overcome. He is the antidote to our weakness, the answer to our need for power.

Harriet Auber, writing over a century ago, gave us the beautiful hymn that enshrines this truth:

> Our blest Redeemer, ere He breathed
>   His tender last farewell,
> A Guide, a Comforter bequeathed
>   With us to dwell.
>
> He came sweet influence to impart,
>   A gracious, willing guest,
> Where he can find one humble heart
>   Wherein to rest.
>
> And every virtue we possess,
>   And every victory won,
> And every thought of holiness,
>   Are His alone.

This promise and consciousness of God living within us is one of the distinctives of Christianity. No other religions offer anything comparable to the Holy Spirit. The presence and power of the Holy Spirit in our lives is a hallmark of the Christian. "The Holy Spirit is the secret of both power and poise," writes E. Stanley Jones. Our Lord made a marvelous provision for us in giving the Holy

we not miss receiving this His highest
holiest gift for us.

———⟊———

*Thank You, Lord, that Your precious
promise of the Holy Spirit is for me as well
as for the disciples in that Upper Room.*

13

The Prayer in the Upper Room

Jesus . . . lifted up His eyes to heaven,
and said . . .—John 17:1

What an experience it must have been to hear Jesus speak or teach! But how most unforgettable to have heard Him pray. The prayer of Jesus in the Upper Room as recorded in John 17 is one of the high watermarks of the Bible.

This is truly the "Lord's Prayer." We could more accurately term the prayer of Matthew 6 the "disciple's prayer." Jesus would soon depart this earthly life. Those who had listened to His sublime words would also pass from the scene. But the words of this prayer will live on forever.

This prayer has been called His high priestly prayer. It is a prayer of intercession with three major petitions. First, Jesus prayed that God would be glorified through His own ministry: "Glorify Your Son, that Your Son also may glorify You" (v. 1). This prayer was abundantly answered by the glory of the cross that has come to "tower o'er the wrecks of time."

Second, He prayed for the disciples: "Keep them from the evil one. . . . Sanctify them" (vv. 15, 17). He prayed that they would not be lost and that they would be fully set apart and cleansed for the tasks of their discipleship.

Finally as we listen in on His pastoral prayer, we are astonished and deeply moved as we hear Him praying for you and me—those of us who would believe on Him in years to come: "[I pray] also for those who will believe in Me through their word" (v. 20). Each of us, in deep devotion, should say, "That was my Lord, and He was praying for me."

He prayed for our unity, that we "may be one" (v. 23). This beautiful prayer should help us do away with our divisiveness and schisms. Sometimes it seems a travesty for a small rural community to have two churches across the road from each other, or a city to have several churches on the same block. Our denominationalism has often fragmented the body of Christ. Thank God for the movement toward unity and ecumenism that is at work today.

As we consider the last week of Jesus' earthly life, we learn that He prayed several times—here in the Upper Room, in Gethsemane, and on the cross itself. The life of our Lord was saturated with prayer which itself becomes an eloquent statement to us of the priority of our communion with God.

Albert Orsborn speaks of this truth in memorable verse:

> In the secret of Thy presence,
>   Where the pure in heart may dwell,
> Are the springs of sacred service
>   And a power that none can tell.
> There my love must bring its offering,
>   There my heart must yield its praise,
> And the Lord will come, revealing
>   All the secrets of His ways.
>
> Blessed Lord, to see Thee truly,
>   Then to tell as I have seen,
> This shall rule my life supremely,
>   This shall be the sacred gleam.
> Sealed again is all the sealing,
>   Pledged again my willing heart,
> First to know Thee, then to serve Thee,
>   Then to see Thee as Thou art.

As the disciples of old, so I ask, "Lord, teach me to pray."

14

The Psalm of
the Upper Room

When they had sung a hymn, they went out to
the Mount of Olives.—Matt. 26:30

On this holy night we have listened to our Lord
discourse with His disciples, to His incomparable
teaching, to His moving prayer. Now there is one
more sound that falls on our ears before we leave
the Upper Room. Suddenly all those in the room
rise and burst into song. Matthew and Mark both
record this moment for us: "When they had sung
a hymn, they went out to the Mount of Olives"
(Matt. 26:30; Mark 14:26).

If only we knew the words they sang as the
shadows grew heavy in the dim light of that Upper
Room. Those words would be forever sacred. We
would want to ponder them, meditate upon their
timeless truth, and make them a part of our own
devotional experience. If only we knew what Jesus
sang with His disciples there on that pivotal night.

But we do know the very words Jesus and His
disciples sang. At the Passover meal, the Hallel
Psalms were sung (Ps. 113—118). They were

psalms of praise that every Jewish boy had to memorize. Psalms 113 and 114 were sung near the beginning of the observance, saving Psalms 115 through 118 for a later point. At the end of the feast, the great Hallel Psalm 136 rang out from grateful hearts.

It is a salutary devotional exercise for the Christian to read these psalms and consider the words that were actually on the lips of our Lord as He prepared to go out to Calvary. Together He and the disciples stood and sang words of courage: "The LORD is on my side; I will not fear. What can man do to me? The LORD is for me among those who help me . . . The LORD is my strength and song, and He has become my salvation." Fulfilling prophecy, He intoned, "The stone which the builders rejected has become the chief cornerstone." In confidence they sang, "This is the day the LORD has made; we will rejoice and be glad in it." And in gratitude they exclaimed, "Give thanks to the LORD, for He is good! For His mercy endures forever" (Ps. 118:6-7, 14, 22, 24, 29).

The music of these psalms was the prelude to Calvary. With these words of praise and confidence, Jesus went on His way to the cross. The medley of praise the disciples sang with the One who was there when "the morning stars sang together" is one of the hidden highlights of inspiration in the Bible.

Music is to the soul as air is to the body. It was

Bach who said the purpose of his music "should be none else but the glory of God and the re-creation of the mind." He himself wrote as though God Himself scrutinized every note and phrase, inscribing at the top of his manuscripts *Soli Deo Gloria* (To God alone the glory). Our Lord knew and exercised the devotional expression of music, and for Him it was a source of strength and inspiration as He journeyed to the cross.

Lord who knew the sustenance of psalms and song, lead me to their fresh, sweet springs for renewal and courage.

15
Gethsemane

He went to the Mount of Olives, as He was
accustomed . . . and He knelt down and
prayed.—Luke 22:39, 41

The supper was over. Christ's immortal words had been spoken. He prayed and sang the psalms of praise in the Upper Room. Then our Lord and the disciples went out into the night.

Together they walked across the Kidron Valley. The brook flowing through the valley that night was running red with the blood of the Passover lambs which had been sacrificed. The blood drained from the altar through a channel that led down to the brook of Kidron. As Jesus crossed this brook, no doubt the thought of His own sacrifice became more vivid in His mind.

Across the brook, He led the disciples to the Garden of Gethsemane. The gospel narrators tell us that this was a familiar retreat for the Master when he notes that Jesus went to Gethsemane ". . . as He was accustomed."

For our Lord, praying in this garden was not an isolated event. Luke tells us it was as usual, or as translated in the King James Version, "as His custom was." Those four words occur only twice in reference to Christ, here and in Luke 4:16. Both times His custom concerned prayer. Jesus prayed instinctively and habitually both in the solitude of communion as well as in public worship.

As Christians, we should not reserve prayer for emergencies; it is to be a vital and regular part of our lives. Prayer sustains and invigorates the spiritual life. Prayer is part and parcel of the Christian life, the intimate companion of consecration.

There is no scene like this in all history. Amid the shadows and agonies of Gethsemane, Jesus fought a battle, the like of which there had never been. The salvation of the world hung in the balance as the tempter sought to deflect Him from the cross. Here with the forces of good and evil locked in deadly combat, Christ took on His armor of prayer. In His supreme hour of trial, crushed under the awful weight of the sins of the world, He poured out His soul in prayer.

To His sleeping disciples, He pleads, "Watch and pray, lest you enter into temptation. The spirit indeed is willing, but the flesh is weak" (Matt. 26:41). This word of our Lord in Gethsemane becomes the watchword for each of us. We all stand in the need of prayer, lest we fall and suffer defeat.

In the city of Cracow, Poland, legend has it that every day for more than seven hundred years a bugle has sounded from the steeple of a particular church. Always the last note is muted, as though some disaster has overtaken the bugler. This ritual commemorates a heroic trumpeter who one day summoned the people to defend themselves against the armies of the invading Tartars. As he was sounding the last note on his trumpet, an arrow from one of the Tartars struck and killed him, thus, the muffled note at the end.

In the Garden of Gethsemane, Jesus sounded the bugle to pray. Surrounded by enemies who were ready to put Him to death, He spoke to His closest followers, the warning: "Watch and pray." Down through the ages He continues to sound this warning to His followers to save us from the enemy of our souls. The lesson of Gethsemane is the lesson of prayer.

———〰———

Christ of Gethsemane, make me adequate for life's tests and crises through the power of prayer.

16
A Lonely
Prayer

Then Jesus came with them to a place called
Gethsemane, and said to the disciples, "Sit here
while I go and pray."—Matt. 26:36

As we follow our Lord to Gethsemane, we feel
constrained to enter this sacred garden on our
knees.

Today the pilgrim to Jerusalem can go to the very
garden believed to have been Gethsemane. The
gnarled, twisted olive trees have been there for two
thousand years, and some of them may very well
have been trees under which the Master prayed. The
pilgrim will pause and pray in such a place, for it is
sacred to the believer. Here our Lord fought the battle for salvation on our behalf, and here He received
strength to endure the cross for us.

Gethsemane is above all a lesson in prayer for
the believer. There our Lord wrestled in prayer as
He felt the terrible weight He must bear of the
"iniquity of us all" (Isa. 53:4–6). Gethsemane is
for each of us a sacred shrine of the soul.

Our Lord's prayer in the garden was a lonely
prayer. "Sit here while I go and pray over there,"

He said to His disciples (Matt. 26:36). Up to a certain point he took Peter, James, and John with Him. But beyond that point He left His dearest ones to journey alone into the deepest depths of His soul's struggle and pilgrimage.

When Jesus returned to His disciples, He found them sleeping and said, "Could you not watch with Me one hour?" Again for a second and third time He went a short distance from them and found them sleeping each time He returned (Matt. 26:40–45). Alone He wrestled with the agony and the fierce life and death struggle of Gethsemane.

There is a difference between loneliness and solitude. We all need solitude; Jesus sought it often. As Wordsworth observed, "The world is too much with us." We look for occasional retreats from our immersion in the tumult of voices, noise, and confusion of the world around us.

Heavy trouble usually involves a call to loneliness. The greatest crises and decisions of life often must be faced alone. Loneliness is an agonizing solitude. In times of trouble we want someone with us. In Gethsemane Jesus had to bear the burden of man's sin and the impending cross alone. As Ben H. Price has expressed it in song:

> It was alone the Savior prayed
> In dark Gethsemane.
> Alone He drained the bitter cup
> And suffered there for me.

Alone, alone, He bore it all alone;
He gave Himself to save His own,
He suffered, bled and died alone, alone.

━━〰━━

Christ of Gethsemane's lonely shadows,
help me to know that I am never alone as
long as You are in my heart.

17
A Sorrowful Prayer

"My soul is exceedingly sorrowful,
even to death."—Matt. 26:38

The language of Scripture hints at a struggle too intense for description. It states, "His sweat became like great drops of blood falling down to the ground" (Luke 22:44). "My heart is breaking" is His poignant cry (Matt. 26:38 PHILLIPS). Our Lord's prayer in Gethsemane was one of indescribable sorrow and agony.

Our Lord's sorrow in Gethsemane was a spiritual one—"My soul is overwhelmed with sorrow," He cried. The soul can experience an anguish deeper than any physical pain. Anguish that pierces the heart wounds more severely than any physical suffering.

The words "even to death" indicate the intensity of our Lord's suffering. He was only thirty-three years old, in the prime of His life. No one wants to die at thirty-three. The shadow of death beneath the olive trees in Gethsemane was a dreaded specter that filled His soul with torment.

"Father, if it is Your will, take this cup away from Me" (Luke 22:42) is our Lord's plea. But He goes on to pray, "Not My will, but Yours, be done." The bitter ingredient of this cup was not fear. Martyrs learned their valor from the One who refused an opiate on the cross.

The bitter taste of the cup of suffering came from betrayal, rejection, calumny, and the wrath of God upon the world's sin. Isaiah prophesied that "the LORD has laid on Him the iniquity of us all" (53:6). Christ had made the long journey from creation to Calvary to "taste death for everyone" (Heb. 2:9).

In our pilgrimage of life, we too may have to pass through a Garden of Gethsemane. Poet Ella Wheeler Wilcox eloquently brings home to us this truth:

In golden youth when seems the earth,
    A summer-land of singing mirth,
When souls are glad and hearts are light,
    And not a shadow lurks in sight.
We do not know it, but there lies,
    Somewhere veiled under evening skies,
A Garden which we all must see—
    The Garden of Gethsemane.

All those who journey, soon or late,
    Must pass within the garden's gate;

Must kneel alone in darkness there,
  And battle with some fierce despair.
God pity those who cannot say,
  "Not mine, but thine," who only pray,
"Let this cup pass," and cannot see
  The purpose in Gethsemane.

How reassuring that when we pass through the sorrowful experiences of life, we have One who understands our sorrows and is there to help and give us victory.

—⁓—

Man of Sorrows, help me to know that You are always standing in the shadows of my life, that You care and understand and are there to help.

18

The Unseen Presence

And He said, "Abba, Father, all things are possible for You."—Mark 14:36

In the moving prayer of our Lord in the garden, we sense not only His loneliness and anguish but also His awareness of the Father's presence. Though forsaken by followers and friends and those dearest to Him, our Lord did not lose sight of His Heavenly Father's nearness to Him in that hour.

Abba is the word Jesus used to address His Father in prayer. There is a note of endearment in this word that is hidden from our Western culture. The early church fathers tell us that Jesus' use of *Abba* to address God is without parallel in all of Jewish literature. The word *Abba* is still used today by a young child in addressing his father, much as a child of our culture would call his father, "Daddy." *Abba* was an everyday family word that no one would have ventured to use for God. But Jesus did. In His hour of desperate need, He spoke to His Father in a childlike, trusting, and intimate way.

"My Father," was the cry of His heart. In His utter loneliness and deep sorrow He did not lose sight of His Father's love and care. We too can know the loving presence of our Heavenly Father when we must pass through the difficult places of life. We, with John Greenleaf Whittier, can say with confidence:

> I know not where His islands lift
> Their fronded palms in air;
> I only know I cannot drift
> Beyond His love and care.

It is better to walk in the dark with God than to run in the light alone. Phillips gives us a paraphrase of Philippians 4:5 which should be indelibly inscribed on each believer's heart: "Never forget the nearness of your Lord." If we will remember in our darkest hour that God is near, that will make all the difference. In this moment of deepest agony, Jesus knew the nearness of His Father's love and care, and that made the difference in the agony and battle of Gethsemane.

—⟋⟍—

Heavenly Father, help me to remember that no matter how dark the night, I am never outside Your love and care.

19

A Triumphant
Prayer

*"Father, if it is Your will, take this cup
away from Me; nevertheless not My will,
but Yours, be done."—Luke 22:42*

We have looked and listened as our Lord has
poured out His soul in His prayer beneath the olive
trees of Gethsemane. He prayed, returned to where
He left His disciples, found them sleeping, chided
them, and as the gospel narrator records, "A second time, He went away and prayed" (Matt. 26:42).
Still the light did not break through the storm's
savage fury, and we see Him returning to His soli-
tary prayer place a third time. Only then did the
calm succeed the storm.

There are answers that will come to us only as
the fruit of persevering prayer. Do we persevere in
our praying for the salvation of a loved one? For
our own sanctification? For the needs of God's
work today? In Gethsemane our Lord teaches us
the lesson of persevering prayer.

"Not My will, but Yours, be done," is the prayer
we hear Him offer in the garden. Is there any
prayer as hard to offer as this one that requires the

surrender of our will to the will of God? Our will dies a stubborn death. But in His will alone is our peace, our victory.

With this prayer of submission the battle in Gethsemane was won—the greatest battle in the history of the world. There the victory of the cross and the resurrection was assured in that prayer of consecration.

We cannot but note the contrast between Christ and His disciples. When Jesus prayed, the disciples slept. Consequently they reaped failure and defeat. His slumbering disciples were not ready for the test and crisis that lay ahead.

Prayer is pivotal for all of us. A prayerless life is a powerless life. A prayerful life is a powerful life. Most of the casualties in the spiritual life are found at the place of a weakened prayer life. In prayer our weakness is linked to divine power, our foolishness joined to eternal wisdom, our need connected with the channel of infinite resources.

The lesson of Gethsemane is the lesson of prayer. We must all watch and pray lest we fall into temptation, and lest the great opportunities for God's kingdom come and pass by, unseen and unseized. With Charles Wesley let us earnestly petition:

> Help me to watch and pray,
> And on Thyself rely,

Assured, if I my trust betray,
I shall for ever die.

———∿———

Divine Helper of men, I will put on the armor of prayer to be adequate for life's tasks and its warfare.

20

The Storm
in the Garden

"Rise, let us be going."—Matt. 26:46

The gathering storm now breaks forth in all its fury. Jesus rises from His prayer in the Garden and announces, "Rise, let us be going!" The words fell from His lips barely a moment before the silence, the solitude, the struggle of Gethsemane were ruthlessly invaded. Matthew records, "While He was still speaking, behold, Judas, one of the twelve, with a great multitude with swords and clubs, came from the chief priests and elders of the people" (Matt. 26:47).

The full moon was high at Passover. Yet John's account describes the multitude as coming with lanterns and torches (18:3). They must have thought Jesus would be hiding and that they would have to search for Him among the trees, shadows, and rocks of the garden.

But when the crowd comes upon the company in the garden, far from hiding, Jesus steps forward and demands, "Whom are you seeking?" When they say, "Jesus of Nazareth," He replies, "I am He" (John 18:4–5).

The crowd, perhaps hundreds of men, came armed to seize Him. The Man they thought would be skulking and hiding now stood before them in reckless candor. In this dramatic moment we observe the courage of Jesus.

Roles suddenly seem reversed. The One they came to capture is in command. An authority radiates from Him that makes the horde fall back. In this dynamic moment we see the charisma of Jesus.

He says to the mob, "I am He. . . . Let these go their way" (John 18:8). His thought is not for His own safety but for that of His followers. In this devoted moment we realize the concern of Jesus.

Peter draws his sword and comes to the defense of his Master. He is willing to lay down his life. But Jesus rebukes him: "Put your sword into the sheath. Shall I not drink the cup which My Father has given Me?" (v. 11). In this decisive moment we sense the commitment of Jesus.

Crisis brings out the true character of a person. It reveals the true self and tests the foundations of life. The crisis of the arrest in the Garden of Gethsemane brought forth the majesty and mercy, the poise and power of Christ. May we so live in fellowship and harmony with our heavenly Father that when the tests of life come our way we will be adequate.

Lord, who stood with calm and strength when hell's forces assailed, give to me the inner strength that will enable me to triumph in the time of testing.

21

Arrest
in the Garden

They came and laid hands on Jesus and took
Him.—Matt. 26:50

The mob that burst upon that sacred scene of
Gethsemane was unusually diverse. Judas led the
pack. Judas, who had been one of the inner circle
of Christ. Judas, who had heard the incomparable
parables, witnessed the mighty miracles, dwelt in
the presence of Love Incarnate, Judas guided the
mob who came to take Christ to His death.

Chief priests and elders were among the leaders
of the mob. They were the very men entrusted
with the sacred duties of the temple and the holy
things of God.

Unfolding in the garden was a drama that grips
our soul's imagination. The mob shouted angrily.
Their lanterns and torchlights broke the darkness.
Flashing in the light were the blades of their swords
and knives, ready to do violence and shed blood.

In the tense and explosive moment, Peter drew
his sword, ready to resist to the death. He swung
it at the nearest enemy to cut off his head. He

barely missed and the man's ear fell to the ground. The whole scene was ready to explode in violence and death.

But again we look at the Man they came to arrest. Once more we see that He was in command. In this mad scene Jesus was an oasis of serenity and sanity. It is His voice and authority that saved the moment from disaster. He commanded His disciples to put up their swords, "for all who take the sword will perish by the sword" (Matt. 26:52). He knew that violence breeds violence.

And the One who had spoken only a short time before of His peace changed this raging storm into calm. He brought peace to this scene of violence. Swords and knives disappeared into their scabbards. And the Son of God, disallowing violence, left willingly in the hands of the mob that was bent on His destruction.

Hiding and watching from the shadows was an unnamed follower of Christ. Mark's account records this dramatic detail: "There happened to be a young man among Jesus' followers who wore nothing but a linen shirt. They seized him, but he left the shirt in their hands and took to his heels stark naked" (Mark 14:51–52 PHILLIPS).

Could this young man have been John Mark himself? That would explain the mystery of his detailed account of what happened at the Gethsemane experience. Could it be that a boy in whose home the Last Supper was held followed

Jesus and His disciples to the garden retreat with just a linen night shirt over him? (How natural for a child to slip out to see something going on instead of going to bed!) Could it be that John Mark then stood in the shadows and saw the scene that seared itself on his memory?

Mark's record of this incident may have been his way of inserting his signature and saying, "When I was a boy I was there. I saw it all happen." And what he saw and experienced there made him later take up his pen and give to the world its earliest account of Jesus Christ.

When we truly encounter the suffering of the Son of God on our behalf, we can never again be the same. Such amazing love overwhelms us with awe, wonder, and adoration.

——⁓⁓——

Man of Sorrows, help me always to remember that I have a God who has known our infirmities, endured our pain and suffering, and bore the agony and separation of death.

22
Amid the Hostile Crowd

*Peter followed at a distance. Now when they
had kindled a fire in the midst of the courtyard
and sat down together, Peter sat among
them.—Luke 22:54–55*

The arresting mob led Jesus to the courtyard
of the high priest. Matthew records: "But Peter
followed Him at a distance to the high priest's
courtyard. And he went in and sat with the servants to see the end" (26:58). John adds that a
disciple, evidently John himself, was allowed to
enter the house (18:15–16). Constrained by love
and devotion, they followed on the fringe of the
crowd, in the poignant words of Matthew, "to see
the end."

It is during these early trials before the Jewish
leaders that the dramatic scene in the courtyard
with Peter took place. Since the garden incident
where Peter cut off the ear of the high priest's
slave, Peter was a marked man. His very presence
in the high priest's courtyard was an act of courage.

The night air had a chill in it, and Peter warmed
himself at the courtyard fire. A servant girl looked
at his tense face reflected in the light of the flames,

then voiced her suspicion that he was one of the disciples. In that moment this stalwart disciple, who just a short time ago was ready to take on the whole mob, cowered before a girl's inquisitive gaze.

Three times Peter was challenged and three times he vehemently denied and disowned his Lord. Then he heard the rooster crow. In that moment, "The Lord turned and looked at Peter. Then Peter remembered the word of the Lord, how He had said to him, 'Before the rooster crows, you will deny Me three times.' So Peter went out and wept bitterly" (Luke 22:61–62).

The loving look of our Lord pierced Peter's heart as a sword and he staggered out into the night and wept bitterly. We are reminded that the penalty of sin is to face not only the anger of Jesus but His unfailing love when we deny Him. But "godly sorrow" leads to repentance, and Peter was later restored by the love and compassion of Christ.

We all readily identify with Peter when Jean Hogan Dudley writes:

As Peter loved I love, and in his fashion,
With boastful promises and bursts of passion;
Then anxious waverings and hot denials,
And faith that drowns amid a sea of trials.
Yet strong beyond my fitful love I see His love
    forever reaching out to me.

Many examples have come to us through history of those like Peter's whose loyalty to Christ was tested under dangerous circumstances. Martin Luther was on his way to the Diet of Worms in 1521. Friends reminded Luther of Jan Hus who was burned at the stake, and advised him not to go. But Luther took his stand before the world's pomp and power. When ordered to recant his statements against the papacy, he replied with words of courage that are engraved in Christian history: "Here I stand; I can do no other, God help me."

In our own time, Dietrich Bonhoeffer paid the cost of discipleship when he resisted Hitler's gross inhumanity. And an innumerable company have resisted the godless persecution at the hands of communism, suffering the penalty of the labor camps and sometimes death. It is said that more Christians have been martyred for their faith in our time than in all previous generations combined.

There comes to each of us a moment when Christ is on trial, when we will be called on to be identified as His followers. We will need courage to stand for Him in a hostile world. Our loyalty to Christ will be challenged. We, too, will be called upon to pay the cost of discipleship.

In the time of testing, let us be sure we are not warming ourselves by the wrong fire. Let us keep in the right company and have our hearts set aglow by the fire of the Holy Spirit. The Master looks at us as He looked at Peter and sees not only our weakness and failure, but our potential to become the faithful followers that He can use for His glory.

The cost of following Christ has never been lowered. There are no discounts or bargains for discipleship. We need to pray with the hymn writer:

In the hour of trial, Jesus plead for me,
  Lest by base denial I depart from Thee;
When Thou seest me waver, With a look recall
  Not for fear or favor, suffer me to fall.

—m—

Lord, in my hour of trial, keep me faithful by Your grace and power.

23

Before Corrupt Annas

The Jews arrested Jesus and bound Him. And they led Him away to Annas first, for he was the father-in-law of Caiaphas who was high priest that year.—John 18:12-13

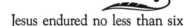

Jesus endured no less than six trials, notorious for being the greatest travesties of justice in all history.

Here we come upon one of the paradoxes of our salvation. The One who came to free us allowed Himself to be taken prisoner. The only One who could offer mercy to humanity—though we've rebelled against the Sovereign of the universe—was going to be tried as a rebel against the religious laws of His day. The One who someday will come to be the Judge of all the earth was tried as a criminal.

The first of the six separate trials takes place before Annas, father-in-law of Caiaphas, the high priest. Annas had amassed a fortune through the exploitation and extortion of worshipers in the sacrifice system of the temple. The shops that sold animals for sacrifice were called the Bazaars of Annas. He himself had been high priest in the time when, in collaboration with Rome, the office went to the highest bidder. When Jesus drove out the money changers from the temple, he had hit Annas where it hurt—his pocketbook. Jesus' righteous anger was a frontal assault on Annas' vested interest.

To Annas, Jesus was a meddling, disturbing Galilean. In his corruption, Annas condemned Jesus even before He was tried.

Today there is a danger of the vested interest of institutional religion conflicting with the claims of Christ. Though we are reluctant to admit it, Christ's presence disturbs our systems—the enterprises we have created in the name of religion.

Too often we have been concerned about the comforts of religion more than the cross, the supper room more than the Upper Room, preached about the perquisites more than the prerequisites.

The prosperity religion espoused by many today seems to have some kinship with Annas and Caiaphas and their cohorts. Let us not relegate old Annas to the archives as a mere curiosity of the Gospels. He keeps appearing in different guises on the scene of history. Luther met him in the form of Tetzel, the corrupt priest. His counterparts visit our living rooms via the marvel of electronics in the form of slick preachers who pull at heartstrings and purse strings. Such men and women who exploit religion for gain are far from Christ and His call to the cross.

*Lord, as I trace Your footsteps to Calvary,
I pray that You will save me from seeking
comfort instead of the cross.*

24
The Charge

The chief priests, the elders, and all the council sought false testimony against Jesus to put Him to death.—Matt. 26:59

Jesus left the house of Annas and was taken to the Sanhedrin, the supreme court of the Jews. It was set up of scribes, Pharisees, Sadducees, and elders—seventy-one members in all. The High Priest, Caiaphas, presided over it.

The Sanhedrin did not have the authority to issue a verdict for execution. Only the Roman governor could hand down the death penalty. But the Sanhedrin met to formulate a charge against Jesus in order to take him before the Roman tribunal. They made their trumped-up charge by maliciously misinterpreting Jesus' statement that the temple would be destroyed and rebuilt in three days. Whereas Jesus had referred to the temple of His body and His resurrection, the Jews sought to charge Him with plotting to destroy the temple at Jerusalem.

"But Jesus kept silent" (Matt. 26:63). This is one of those sublimely eloquent silences of Jesus.

The silences of Jesus were as authoritative as His sermons. As in our day, no person on trial could be compelled to answer any question that would incriminate him, so Jesus' silence was within the provision of the law.

Then the High Priest played his trump card. "Are you the Messiah?" he demanded. "Are you the Son of God?" All the universe held its breath awaiting the answer to this question. He had only to say no and the case against Him would fail. To say yes would be to sign His own death warrant before this group. Jesus answered yes and quoted Daniel 7:13, which describes His ultimate triumph as the Son of God.

In hysterical horror, the members of the Sanhedrin tore their garments, cried "Blasphemy!" and demanded the death sentence. Their venomous hatred of Jesus spewed forth as "they spat in His face and beat Him; and others struck Him with the palms of their hands, saying, 'Prophesy to us, Christ! Who is the one who struck You?'" (Matt. 26:67–68). Even the pretense of justice was abandoned in their malice. The trial was a sham—a mere formality to carry out their design for murder.

Jesus was the only sinless person who ever lived on this planet. He whose attribute is holiness and righteousness endured mockery and travesty of justice unparalleled in the history of man. And He did it all for you and me!

*Help me, Lord, when life is unfair or cruel,
to learn from Your sublime example of
courage, poise, and trust.*

25

Caiaphas'
Mockery of Justice

*When morning came, all the chief priests and
elders of the people plotted against Jesus to put
Him to death.—Matt. 27:1*

The Sanhedrin had met illegally at night and
interrogated Jesus in the private house of Caiaphas.
The brief meeting of the Sanhedrin formed the final
official charge of blasphemy (Matt. 27:1-2). From
there they bound Christ and took Him to Pilate.

But these Jewish leaders knew that if they
brought their charge to the Roman governor, he
would tell them to settle their own religious quar-
rels. Thus they fabricated three political charges,
all false: (1) national subversive activity; (2) oppos-
ing payment of taxes; (3) claiming to be a king
(Luke 23:2). They knew these charges would be
considered treasonous in a court of the Roman
Empire trying to maintain order in the highly vola-
tile Jewish provinces.

The Sanhedrin had very strict regulations. All
criminal cases had to be tried. They could not hear
criminal cases during festival seasons. Only if the
verdict were "not guilty" could a case be concluded

on the day it began. No decision of the Sanhedrin was valid unless its members gathered in the Sanhedrin's own meeting place, the Hall of Hewn Stone in the temple precincts. All evidence had to be substantiated by two witnesses separately examined and having no contact with each other. The penalty for false testimony was death. The court had to hear supporting evidence for the innocence of the accused before considering the evidence of his guilt.

It is blatantly clear that in their plot to eliminate Jesus, the Sanhedrin violated every one of these rules of justice. They met during the night. They transacted the trial during the Passover. They met secretly in the house of the High Priest. They abandoned the rules requiring two witnesses. They heard no evidence on Jesus' behalf.

Here we witness the greatest injustice and mockery of all history. No one else ever walked a road of such sorrow and suffering as did Jesus Christ.

As we ponder the unparalleled sufferings of Christ, we are once again overwhelmed by the amazing love of God that condescended to suffer the rejection, the injustice, the mockery, the malice, and the brutality of men that we may be saved and be with Him forever.

—⚹—

Christ who art the Truth, help me to quit playing games with You and to be honest, truthful, upright, without pretence or falsehood.

26

Before Pilate and Herod

Then they led Jesus from Caiaphas to the Praetorium.—John 18:28

"Suffered under Pontius Pilate" are the familiar words of the Apostles' Creed. To the end of time Pilate will fill that unenviable niche in history. His name might have been synonymous with courage and honor, but instead it is associated with infamy and cowardice.

Political insurrection and rebellion were the most serious charges that could be brought against an offender in any Roman court. From the outset, Pilate apparently recognized Jesus as undeserving of the charges made by the Jews. He saw through their malice and fraud. He tried at least five different strategies to avoid the responsibility of judging Jesus. Right at the start he said to the Jews, "You take Him and judge Him according to your law" (John 18:31).

But the Jews were bent on the death of Jesus, and only Pilate's office could inflict the death sentence. Pilate tried next to transfer the responsibility of judging Jesus to Herod since Galilee was Herod's province. But that didn't work either.

Jesus' appearance before Herod is marked by His silence. Jesus had absolutely nothing to say to Herod. The ruler regarded Jesus merely as a spectacle. He treated our Savior as a joke, putting upon Him a king's robe, jesting and mocking Him and treating Him contemptuously. Again there is eloquence in silence. The man is surely lost who merits nothing but the silence of Jesus.

So the Jews brought Jesus back to Pilate. Pilate's third strategy for avoiding his responsibility was to release a prisoner as an act of mercy during the Passover. But the frenzied mob chose Barabbas. Then Pilate had Jesus scourged, thinking that brutal ordeal would appease their hatred. But it only seemed to incite them all the more to be finished with Jesus. Pilate made a final appeal, but all to no avail.

In each of the two appearances of Christ before him, the Roman governor interrogated Him. Each time, he pronounced his judgment: "I find no fault in Him at all" (John 18:38).

After Pilate had continually vacillated and compromised his conviction, there came that terrible moment when Jesus "gave him no answer." Pilate had conceded to the fanaticism and malice of the crowd and condemned Jesus to the brutal scourging. Then he tried to probe further in questioning Christ about His true identity. But there comes a time when discussion is no longer possible. There is nothing further to be said. Jesus had been silent before the high priest. He was silent before Herod. Now He becomes silent before Pilate. And in that moment Pilate received the terrible judgment of Christ.

Each attempted strategy of the Roman governor had only served to raise the temperature of the seething hatred of the mob. They had now reached that point at which their hatred became insane, lost rationality, and issued forth in hysteria and violence. Such hatred was impervious to reason and mercy. The voices of the shrieking mob howled like wolves in frenzied fanaticism, "Away with Him, away with Him! Crucify Him!" (John 19:15).

Yet the sanctimonious Sanhedrin, the once powerful Pilate and Herod became but pawns in the grand chess game of history as Christ inexorably moved toward God's "checkmate" of sin and Satan.

—⚹—

Help me, Lord, to be responsive where hate calls for love, suffering cries for compassion, and injustice demands my action.

27

"Suffered Under
Pontius Pilate"

*When he had scourged Jesus, he delivered Him
to be crucified.—Matt. 27:26*

Ironically, the same Jews that were demanding
the death of the Son of God had, only a few hours
before, been conducting the meticulous ceremo-
nial search for leaven in their homes as part of the
Passover rite. They wanted to be absolutely certain
not to have anything that would render them un-
clean.

Do you know someone who fusses about the
trifles of religious custom while violating God's law
of love and kindness? It is possible for us to give
the greatest care to the details of our ritual and
neglect the spirit of love and fellowship.

The Jews were not making any real progress in
their mockery of a trial. They had not yet been
able to force Pilate to pronounce the death sentence. But now the Jews came forth with their most
devastating charge, one Pilate could not afford to
ignore: "If you let this man go, you are not Caesar's
friend. Whoever makes himself a king speaks

against Caesar" (John 19:12). Pilate had some previous serious trouble in Palestine that had been reported to Rome. He was in no position to take a risk of such a serious charge as this against his administration. The Jewish leaders blackmailed Pilate. He sympathized with Jesus. But he wanted to keep his power and position. He capitulated to the Jewish leaders and pronounced the dreaded sentence of crucifixion on Jesus.

In Pilate's attempts to avoid making a judgment of Christ, we have a parable of the human soul. Each of us confronts a decision about Christ. We can never delegate our decision to another. We can never work around that responsibility. The question stubbornly haunts us and keeps returning until we decide.

In essence, Pilate was only the tool of the religious leaders of the Jews. But he goes down in history as the one under whom Christ suffered.

There are the awful words of the record: "He had scourged Jesus" (Matt. 27:26). The Gospel narrative says just that and no more. There is a reverent reticence in the Scripture. The writers do not go into the graphics of the scourging, but we know that such scourgings were performed with terrible leather thongs woven with pieces of bone and iron. It was a fearsome ordeal, certain to tear the lacerated flesh to ribbons and often causing death.

After this horrible scourging, Pilate "delivered

Him to be crucified." Christ indeed "suffered under Pontius Pilate."

In this trial we have one of the greatest paradoxes of history. Christ was actually found innocent by the highest court of His day. Yet He was beaten, tortured, and crucified. Pilate sacrificed the Savior on the altar of political expediency in return for the ashes of his personal ambition.

———

Lord, purify my motives so I will not fear Your tampering with my ambitions or pressing Your real claims upon my life.

28
The Moment
of Decision

"What then shall I do with Jesus who is called Christ?"—Matt. 27:22

Throughout the trials we cannot escape the sheer majesty of Jesus Christ. As Pilate floundered in bewilderment, Jesus Christ exhibited a poise and perception that is all the more radiant in contrast. In Jesus' demeanor we see that it was really Pilate who was being judged.

Pilate asked Jesus the probing question, "What is truth?" But in the classic words of Francis Bacon, he "would not stay for an answer." He was blind to the momentous truth that stood before him, unaware that he was addressing Truth Incarnate.

The searching gaze of Jesus as He looked at Pilate reverses their roles. Christ is in reality the Judge, and it is Pilate who is on trial.

When I go to a museum and look at some of the world's great masterpieces of art or sculpture, or listen to a Beethoven symphony, or read a classic piece of literature, I am not judging these immortal works. Rather I am being judged by my response to them. My aesthetics, sensitivity, perception, and disciplines are being judged. In the same way, we never judge Christ, but rather our life is judged by our response to Him.

Pilate had a direct and dramatic confrontation with life's ultimate question: "What then shall I do with Jesus who is called Christ?" Jesus Christ alone confronts us with such a choice. It is not necessary that we make up our mind about Socrates, Napoleon, or Shakespeare. Our opinion concerning any other person in history has little influence upon our lives. But our choice regarding Jesus Christ determines our character and destiny.

Someone has said that the doctrine of election is easy to understand: "God has one vote and that is always for you. Satan has one vote and that is always against you. You have the other vote and that decides the election."

Pilate tried to withdraw from that moral choice by washing his hands to symbolize that he carried no responsibility for the death of Christ. But we cannot be neutral toward Jesus. We have to make a decision between two wash basins—the one of servanthood symbolized by Jesus washing His disciples' feet in the Upper Room or the one of status-seeking symbolized by Pilate's abdication of responsibility.

It is an amazing and awesome thought that the eternal Christ stands at the threshold of my little life. The omnipotent Christ of the universe desires and deigns to live in and through my frail life. And He gives me the choice to accept or reject Him!

On one fall journey my family and I stopped with other tourists to observe the Continental Divide, which goes all the way from Canada to Mexico. We are told that two drops of rain falling just a few inches apart will end up in different oceans. Likewise, there is a great spiritual divide. Some people determine that they will accept Jesus at the eleventh hour, then they die at 10:30. As with Pilate, indecision determines destiny.

Some moments of time hold eternity. Columbus had his supreme moment and seized it for immortality. Washington had his hour that would influence the destiny of the world. And there are moments which come to us with a qualitative content that far transcends their fraction of time. Pilate faced such a moment when Christ stood before him. We face such a moment when we make our choice regarding Christ.

"What then shall I do with Jesus?" is the universal question asked by humankind. It is a question for me. It is a question for you. In our decision is our destiny and fulfillment. Someday we will be asking, "What will Jesus do with me?"

James Russell reminds us in his memorable lines:

> Once to every man and nation
> Comes the moment to decide,

In the strife of truth with falsehood,
For the good or evil side . . .
And the choice goes by forever
'Twixt that darkness and that light.

———∽———

*Come over here, Lord, into my life—
where I have not wanted You to come—
and occupy every corner of my life.*

29

The Via Dolorosa

*And He, bearing His cross, went out to a place
called the Place of a Skull.*—John 19:17

His sentence pronounced, our Lord was compelled to walk the Via Dolorosa, the Road of Sorrows. It is the most sacred road in history. It is the road on which love traveled the farthest. Its stones and dust were stained with the blood of the Son of God. It is the road that bridged the gap between earth and heaven, between man and God. It is the road that led to Calvary.

It was customary for a condemned criminal to be led away to the crucifixion, as was Jesus. The prisoner walked in the center of four Roman soldiers and carried his own cross beam. The charge against him was written on a board hung around the prisoner's neck or carried by a soldier in front of the procession and later affixed to the cross. Crucifixion was the most horrible and cruel death devised for the worst criminals as a punishment for them and a deterrent for others. It would indeed be a grim sight to see a man carrying his death beam to his crucifixion.

Legends concerning this portion of our Lord's Passion abound. One story tells that Jesus, under the exhaustion of carrying the cross, leaned against the door of a house on the road. The occupant struck Him and commanded Him to hurry on. The Lord turned to His assailant and replied, "Thou shalt go on and never stop till I come again." This is the legend of the Wandering Jew who supposedly still moves over the earth, unable to find rest or death. It is, of course, a symbolic representation of the tragic fate of the Jewish people, who—since the day they laid violent hands on the Son of God—have had no rest from wandering the earth.

And there is the legend of Veronica, who, seeing Christ on this road of sorrows, came out of her house and washed away the blood and sweat from His face. When she examined the towel with which the loving act had been performed, she saw a perfect likeness of the Man of Sorrows. This scene has been reproduced by great artists who remind us that the common acts of love in life are stamped with the image of Christ.

Neither of these stories is considered fact. But both capture our attention and challenge our action as we consider the account of the Via Dolorosa, the Road of Sorrows.

As we ponder this most sacred scene, let us ask

ourselves the question and pray the prayer posed
in the hymn of Isaac Watts:

> Am I a soldier of the cross,
>   A follower of the Lamb,
> And shall I fear to own His cause,
>   Or blush to speak His name?
>
> Must I be carried to the skies
>   On flowery beds of ease,
> While others fight to win the prize,
>   And sail through stormy seas?
>
> Since I must fight if I would reign,
>   Increase my courage, Lord!
> I'll bear the toil, endure the pain,
>   Supported by Thy word.

*Christ of the Road of Sorrows, give me a
willingness to pay the cost of true discipleship.*

30

Simon
the Crossbearer

*As they led Him away, they laid hold of a
certain man, Simon a Cyrenian . . . and on
him they laid the cross that he might bear it
after Jesus.—Luke 23:26*

Many a man died from the scourging of the
dreaded Roman cat-o'-nine-tails. But Jesus sur-
vived that harrowing ordeal, as well as the sleepless
night, the quick succession of trials, and the
pointless interrogation. It is incredible that He
could carry the cross at all. Weakened from the
torture, He soon sank beneath the weight of the
death beam as He walked the Road of Sorrows.

Palestine was an occupied country, and a Roman
soldier could press any person into service. He did
so by putting the flat of the blade of a Roman
spear on the person's shoulder. As Jesus faltered,
the soldiers, impatient with the delay, got hold of
Simon, an onlooker, and pressed him into service.
The Pharisees and Roman soldiers were in a hurry
to get this wretched business over with and had
no time to wait for the exhausted prisoner to struggle up the hill. To Simon it must have been an
extreme annoyance, a terrible indignity as a name-

less Roman soldier involves him in the divine drama of the ages.

Mark's account includes a clue to the identity of Simon. Mark describes him as the father of Alexander and Rufus (15:21). Alexander and Rufus must have been well known for them to be identified this way in the text. Here we have one of the hidden romances of the New Testament. Scholars believe that Mark wrote his gospel for the church at Rome. In the greetings of his letter to the church at Rome, Paul writes: "Greet Rufus, chosen in the Lord, and his mother, who has been a mother to me, too" (Rom. 16:13 NIV). Thus we find in the Roman church Rufus, so choice a Christian that he is called one of God's chosen; and his mother so dear to Paul that he calls her his own mother in the Christian faith. It seems very plausible that she could be Simon's wife.

In Acts 13:1 Simeon (another name for Simon) is listed as one of the men of Antioch who sent Paul and Barnabas out on their mission to the Gentiles. In that passage Simeon is also called Niger, and Niger was the name for a man with dark skin from Africa, and Cyrene is in Africa. It is not at all improbable that Simon and Simeon are the same person.

We would like to have heard the story Simon told that day when he returned to his wife and his sons, Alexander and Rufus. Can we not imagine his face aglow as he tells of the rude interruption, his quick resentment, then of the face he would never forget, of the brutal scene of Calvary that was seared on his memory, of the dying love of Christ on the cross! On that road of sorrows and on the skull-shaped hill, Simon felt the irresistible pull of the magnet of Calvary, and his life was never the same again.

Simon of Cyrene's experience is typical of all life. Somewhere on our road of life we too will meet the Master carrying His cross for us. And we too will be given opportunity to share in the fellowship of His suffering and to carry our cross for Him.

It was Dietrich Bonhoeffer who wrote in his *The Cost of Discipleship*, "When Christ calls a man, He bids him come and die." All of us sooner or later must bear a cross. Our crosses are hewn of different woods, but we must all have our Calvaries. Life's true meaning and value lie close to the cross.

Had Simon of Cyrene not borne that cross, we never would have heard of him. He must have looked back to that cross as the greatest event of his life. Because he carried the cross, Simon, his wife, his sons, and others found Christ and eternal life.

We too will find the true meaning of life in carrying our cross for Him. We are challenged by the hymn of Thomas Shepherd and G. N. Allen:

Must Jesus bear the cross alone
  And all the world go free?
No, there's a cross for everyone,
  And there's a cross for me.
The consecrated cross I'll bear
  Till death shall set me free;
And then go home my crown to wear,
  For there's a crown for me.

*Christ, my crossbearer, help me to take up
my cross daily and follow You.*

31
The Women
Who Wept

A great multitude of the people followed Him,
and women who also mourned and lamented
Him.—Luke 23:27

We have been sated with horrors as we have
considered the suffering of Christ through His Passion. At times it seems we have been more among
demons than men. Our mind longs for some relief
from this spectacle of fanatic hate and cold-
blooded cruelty. And suddenly on this path of woe
there is a blink of sunshine, and our faith in human
kindness and love is renewed.

It is Luke who gives us this portrait of women
mourning and wailing for Christ as He was
hounded on His way to execution. The women of
Jerusalem paid the tribute of their tears to the
suffering of the Son of God. Jewish law forbade
showing sympathy to a condemned man. But the
outpouring of their compassion was too strong to
be held back by the walls of law and custom.

With all the record of opposition to Jesus, there
is no instance written of in which a woman op-
posed Christ. No women ever forsook, betrayed,

or in any way expressed enmity against Christ. Rather they followed Him, opened to Him their homes and hearts, bathed His feet with their tears, anointed His head with perfume, and now, as men dragged Him to His death, they showed the compassion of their sorrow and wept for Him on His way to martyrdom.

Jesus today still needs from women their compassion and tears, not for Himself but for those who are carrying heavy crosses that have been unfairly thrust upon them. They will be crushed beneath the weight of those crosses unless someone cares and weeps and loves.

Women can give the compassion that can keep the heart of the world from hardening. Their sensitivities are needed more than ever in this day of depersonalization and creeping anonymity. God has beautifully and uniquely endowed women. The compassion and tenderness that they are able to give are deeply needed by our suffering world today. In this age of high-tech we need the help and healing of high-touch.

Jesus turned to the women and said, "Daughters of Jerusalem, do not weep for Me, but weep for yourselves and for your children" (Luke 23:28). At the very moment when His body was wracked by the pain of the scourging and the weight of the cross and His mind tortured with the approach of still more terrible agonies, He turned from His own suffering to what He knew would be in store for those women. He foreknew the terrible fate of Jerusalem that was less than half a century away. The coming destruction of Jerusalem was unparalleled in its horror. Josephus, the historian, describes it: "There has never been a race on earth, and there never will be one, whose sufferings can be matched with those of Jerusalem in the days of the siege."

Jesus poignantly prophesies here again the doom so soon to befall the people of Jerusalem. The suffering of the women and children, especially through starvation, was one of the horrors of the siege. For centuries and still today, representatives of the Jewish race go to the Wailing Wall every Friday to weep over the destruction of their city and temple in A.D. 70.

In this glimpse through a narrow window of Luke's gospel we see the extraordinary compassion of Christ and an eloquent expression of the love that many of the common people had for the Master. Albert Orsborn in his song reminds us of our need for the compassion of Christ:

The Savior of men came to seek and to save
    The souls who were lost to the good;
His spirit was moved for the world which he
    loved
    With the boundless compassion of God.
And still there are fields where the laborers
    are few,
    And still there are souls without bread,

And still eyes that weep where the darkness is
    deep,
    And still straying sheep to be led.

Except I am moved with compassion,
How dwelleth thy spirit in me?
    In word and in deed
    Burning love is my need;
I know I can find this in thee.

—⟋⟋⟍—

Save me, Lord, from ever being an individ-
ual island of life, untouched by divine
commandment and human need. Give to
me a heart of compassion that will weep
for the lost and hurting.

32

The Silence of Calvary

He was oppressed and He was afflicted,
Yet He opened not His mouth.—Isa. 53:7.

We now come to consider the end of Christ's earthly journey. We have followed Him down the Road of Sorrows, which has come to its end on Golgotha's hill. Strange place indeed for God Incarnate to end His earthly mission. He had created all the unspeakably beautiful places upon this earth. Yet He made His earthly exit from this ugly place of execution, outside the gate of the city. As George MacLeod put it:

Jesus was not crucified in a cathedral between two candles, but on a cross between two thieves: on the town garbage-heap; at a crossroad so cosmopolitan that they had to write His title in Hebrew, Latin, and Greek; at the kind of place where cynics talk smut, and thieves curse, and soldiers gamble. Because that is where He died. And that is what He died about. And that is where churchmen should be and what churchmanship should be about.

We often ponder the last words of Christ from the cross, but overall there was an awesome silence at Calvary. Jesus spoke only seven times during the six hours of the crucifixion, a total of only forty-one words in His original language. All together those seven utterances took less than one minute. Thus, for five hours and fifty-nine minutes He said nothing at all. This was not due to physical weakness, for the Gospel narrators tell us that more than once He spoke with a loud voice.

Centuries earlier, Isaiah wrote as though he were standing at the foot of the cross: "He was oppressed and He was afflicted, Yet He opened not His mouth; he was led as a lamb to the slaughter, And as a sheep before its shearers is silent, So He opened not His mouth" (Isa. 53:7). The fact that God inspired Isaiah, the great prophet of the suffering of Christ, to prophesy the silence of the cross is an indication that Christ's silence on Calvary was not merely a consequence of suffering but held a sacred significance.

Would not the cross have been a powerful pulpit? What a setting the cross would have been for proclaiming some of His great truths such as John 3:16. Yet Jesus was mostly silent during these final hours when the great fountain of salvation was being opened for the world.

The preacher of Ecclesiastes gives us one of the reasons for Christ's silence when he states that there is "a time to keep silence, and a time to speak" (3:7). The cross was a time for sacred silence. Sometimes silence speaks louder than thunder; sometimes its cries are sharper than a two-edged sword; sometimes it is more powerful than a marching army. Often the deepest experiences of life would only be diminished by words.

A second reason has to do with the scene of Calvary and those who were a part of it. As Jesus was dying on the cross, many of the onlookers made sport of His suffering. They jeered and jested at the Son of God upon the cross. Jesus would not cast His "pearls before swine." His enemies at the cross showed nothing but contempt for His suffering. They did not get a single word from Jesus, only the rebuke of silence. A mere man might have tried to say something in this situation. But the Son of God's silence was more eloquent than any words.

The words of Jesus carried authority. So did His silences. Following his denial, Peter was restored not with any word of condemnation, but with a silent glance that penetrated the depths of his soul. We have seen that before Caiaphas Jesus held His peace; before Herod He never said a word. Pilate marvelled at the quiet fortitude of Jesus. From the silence of Christ on the cross comes the powerful truth of the eternal significance of that moment.

In contrast we hear His few sublime words spoken to the faithful and the penitent. When we come to Him, with a contrite heart or as a faithful follower, then we too will hear His gracious word spoken to the prayerful and penitent soul.

—◊—

Master, speak to me by name and need that
I may follow closer in Your steps.

33

The Seven
Sayings

But He was wounded for our transgressions,
He was bruised for our iniquities;
The chastisement for our peace was upon Him,
And by His stripes we are healed.—Isa. 53:5

The final words of the world's great men are
often chronicled in the books and libraries of the
world or engraved upon marble and monuments.
But these last seven statements of Jesus are indelibly engraved upon the heart of every Christian.
They are held in highest reverence and deepest
devotion. These seven sayings are like seven win-
dows in the Savior's mind and soul during His hour
of supreme suffering.

To contemplate these words is a spiritually transforming experience. Bishop Ambrose preached on
these words on a Good Friday over 1,500 years ago.
He ascended his pulpit in Milan and addressed his
congregation with the following words: "I find it
impossible to speak to you today. The events of
Good Friday are too great for human words. Why
should I speak while my Savior is silent and dies?"
John Milton, the poet of towering genius, had
much the same experience when he tried to write

a poem about Calvary, called *The Passion*. He put it away after writing just a few stanzas and never returned to it. On his working manuscript was found this footnote: "This subject the author finds to be above his years he had, and nothing satisfied with what was begun, he left it unfinished." Part of his unfinished work reveals how he felt:

My sorrows are too dark for day to know,
  The leaves should all be black whereon I
    write,
And letters where my tears had washed a
    wannest white.

Every preacher and every writer who has ever seriously sought to address this subject knows something of Milton's experience. All our words are utterly weak and inadequate when we encounter the majesty and might and mercy of those seven utterances from the cross. These seven statements usher us into the Holy of Holies in the suffering and great salvation of God for sinful men.

No other event of all history has had such an impact upon us as Calvary. We do not feel a part of any other death in history. Other great men died. They have our admiration and become part of our history lessons, but that is all. It is surpassingly different with the crucifixion of Jesus Christ. We feel very much a part of Calvary and the cross and all that happened there. When Rembrandt painted the crucifixion, among the faces in the crowd the great artist painted himself, knowing he was a part of that divine drama of the ages. Yes, we were there. Our sins were the tongues that jeered Him, the palms that slapped Him, the knuckled fists that pummelled His face. Our sins were the lashes that cut His back to shreds, the thorns that punctured His brow, the nails that pierced His sacred hands, the lance that punctured His side. Our sins were the wagging heads that mocked Him when hanging on the cross. His every breath was a pang of pain, His every heartbeat a throb of agony.

We were there when they crucified our Lord, represented by our sin and the mighty salvation He accomplished for us. His sacred words and His sublime sacrifice were for me and you and all the world.

———

Divine Love, impaled upon a cross, I am moved to a holy hush and a deeper devotion as I contemplate the sacred scene of Calvary.

34

The Word of Forgiveness

"Father, forgive them, for they do not know what they do."—Luke 23:34

Jesus' first word from the cross was, "Father." His first utterance was a prayer: "Father, forgive them, for they do not know what they do."

When righteousness seemed trampled underfoot and wrong triumphant, when He was being put to death by His enemies, when His fortunes were at their blackest, when His body quivered with the pain of the flogging and the spikes of the cross and His soul felt the even sharper sword of desertion and betrayal, when every breath was a pain and every heartbeat an agony, Jesus still was able to say, "Father."

This utterance to heaven from Golgotha is the highest reach of faith known to man. When it seemed God's hand was withdrawn from the rudder of the universe, Jesus called out to His Father. It was an acknowledgment of the authority of God in spite of the anarchy of men. It evoked the presence of God in life's most desolate moment. It testified to the love of God triumphant over the violence of man. It witnessed to the faithfulness of God in the face of man's faithlessness. It demonstrated the care of God amid life's cruelty and callousness.

This first word of the cross reminds us that when life comes tumbling down, we too may know the unfailing presence of God our Father. It assures us we need never bear life's crosses alone.

Tradition has it that this first saying from the cross was spoken as the soldiers were driving the spikes through our Lord's hands and feet. At Calvary Jesus added His own powerful example to His command, "Love your enemies and pray for those who persecute you." The teachings and the example of Jesus beautifully intersected at Calvary. Now man could not relegate His teaching to a great ideal or utopian dream. Jesus' words are immortal because He realized their challenge even under the most severe trials.

"To err is human, to forgive divine," wrote Alexander Pope. Forgiveness on a human level is one of life's highest qualities. It never comes easily. It often costs dearly. Perhaps nothing is as difficult. For the person deeply wronged it is natural to nurse the hurt, to hold on to it for its own bitter protest, to consider revenge a sweet satisfaction. But the first words of Jesus from the cross teach us the sublime lesson of forgiveness.

Lord, You who have forgiven me of so much, enable me always to be forgiving, to live by Your sublime example on Calvary.

35

The Word
of Salvation

*"Assuredly, I say to you, today you will be with
Me in Paradise."—Luke 23:43*

The death of Christ on the cross was God's
grand plan of salvation coming to fruition. Yet
around the cross we find no evidence of a saving
faith. The few faithful gathered at Calvary were
there in grief, not faith. For the soldiers it was
just another day's work. The onlookers who milled
around challenged Him to come down and save
Himself or joined others who made sport of it all.
The prophecy of Isaiah becomes fulfilled in this
terrible moment: "He is despised and rejected by
men" (Isa. 53:3).

In the midst of this scene of mockery and grief,
suddenly there was one exception, one voice that
sounded a different note! It didn't seem to fit into
that picture of rejection at all. In contrast to the
taunting and ridicule, there came a voice saying,
"Lord, remember me when You come into Your
kingdom" (Luke 23:42).

Who said that? Surely it must have been Mary

or one of the women, or John. But no, not a word came from them, only their inconsolable grief. Perhaps it was the plea of a person whom Jesus had healed. Or perhaps Peter had returned to acknowledge Christ? No, none of these. The words were uttered by the person from whom we would least expect to hear them—a condemned criminal on his own cross next to Jesus, a person whom the world wanted to get rid of, whom they judged unfit to live. And so the distinction of being the only soul who trusted in the crucified Christ for salvation goes to one of the dregs of human society.

The reply of Jesus is the word of salvation. It comes instantly in response to the man's simple faith. This man, forgotten of all others, now would never be forgotten of God.

The Polish astronomer Copernicus' research and writings on the nature of the solar system radically changed man's conception of the universe. On his deathbed, *The Revolution of the Heavenly Bodies*—his great work, just off the press—was laid in his arms. But in that moment as he came face-to-face with life's ultimate fact, he did not think of himself as a great scientist, mathematician, astronomer, or one of the world's most learned men. He thought of himself as a sinner in need of the grace and salvation of Christ on the cross. His faith and prayer are expressed in the epitaph he wrote for himself which can be read today on his grave: "Lord I do not ask the kindness which

Thou didst show to Peter. I do not dare to ask the grace which Thou didst grant to Paul. But Lord, the mercy Thou didst show to the dying robber, that mercy show to me. That earnestly I crave."

We each may pray the prayer of the penitent thief, and praise God, we each may hear Christ's gracious word of salvation and His promise of life eternal.

——◆——

Dear Savior, as the dying thief in faith looked to You and found forgiveness and eternal life, so I cast myself alone upon the merit of Your infinite sacrifice for me and pray, Lord, remember me.

36
The Word of Love

He said to His mother, "Woman, behold your son!" Then He said to the disciple, "Behold your mother!"—John 19:26–27

The Scriptures tell us that Jesus had brothers and sisters with Him as He grew up (Mark 6:3). We can picture Him taking on the role of the oldest child in the family. Perhaps He helped James and Joses and Judas and Simon and His sisters take their first faltering steps, shepherded them through the village and marketplace, held them back from the racing wheels of chariots or the lumbering wheels of caravans that so often passed through Nazareth.

During those years perhaps He ran errands for his mother, drew water from the well, replenished the fire on a chilly evening. And perhaps on that desolate day when Joseph, the father of that home, was laid to rest, it was He who put strong and comforting arms around His mother. It was He who took over the support of the home, selflessly stepping into Joseph's place at the carpenter bench.

Then came the day when His brothers were old enough to take over the carpentry business and His sisters surrounded Mary with loving care. The silent years were over. For the last time He shook the wood shavings from His tunic, said a tender good-bye to His family, kissed His mother and dried her tears, and turned His back upon Nazareth. The time had come for the Son of God to go forth and accomplish His mighty mission of salvation for the world. As Mary watched Him that day walking down the dusty road that led from their home in Nazareth, she must have wondered what the future would bring for her Son.

So much had happened during the three incredible years that followed. But now His life was all ending in tragedy and ignominy. Her Son, whose life overflowed with love and goodness, was dying a criminal's death in the midst of cruel hatred and violence. Simeon's prophecy was being brutally fulfilled: "A sword will pierce through your own soul also" (Luke 2:35). Now at the foot of the cross, Mary felt the sword's sharp cutting. Those outstretched arms that had hugged her neck as a child were cruelly pierced on that cross. His mouth was parched in dying thirst, and she could not moisten it. The thorns encircling His brow and the mocking taunts flung at Him wounded her also. The suffering of Mary was greater than the suffering of any other person at Calvary, outside the suffering of Jesus Himself.

In that moment Jesus forgot His own torment and unspeakable agony and spoke His words of love to His mother. He asked His closest friend, John, to take His mother as his own. In ten unforgettable words He tells His mother that John was now her son and would care for her. John could not leave this beautiful word and act of compassion from his gospel.

It is John who gives us this record: "Now there stood by the cross of Jesus His mother" (John 19:25). Mary could not have been anywhere else at this moment. For Kipling's famous words were born out of the experience of all humanity:

If I were hanged on the highest hill,
I know whose love would follow me still,
   Mother o'mine, O mother o'mine!
If I were drowned in the deepest sea,
I know whose tears would come down to me,
   Mother o'mine, O mother o'mine!
If I were damned by body and soul,
   I know whose prayers would make me
     whole,
   Mother o'mine, O mother o'mine!

The bond of friendship constrained John to stand at the foot of the cross. It is always painful to take leave of a loved one in the hour of death. The ties of family and friendship are so cruelly severed at death. For those who survive, something very precious goes out of life. For John as well as Mary, this was a moment of deep agony and loss. The disciple whom Jesus loved responded to Jesus' words of compassion, "From that hour that disciple took her to his own home" (John 19:27).

We are a part of the family of God. Together we will have all eternity to grow in that relationship which transcends death and the tragedies of life.

———ᴍ———

Lord, who forgot Your own suffering and exemplified family love on the cross, help me to be tender and responsible in the sacred relationships of my life.

37
The Word
of Abandonment

*"My God, My God, why have You forsaken
Me?"—Mark 15:34*

From the cross next came a cry that astonishes
us and is too deep for our understanding: "My
God, My God, why have You forsaken Me?" It is
a cry of abandonment.

This word from the cross is quoted from the
Messianic prophecy of Psalm 22. That psalm may
well be called the Psalm of the Cross. It portrays
our Savior's final hour, records His dying words,
and is a memorial of His infinite love for the world.
The psalm begins with this fourth saying of Jesus
from the cross. Thus Christ was identifying Himself with this prophecy. As the Messiah He was
accomplishing on the cross our salvation from sin
and its penalty.

In this moment Jesus felt the utter loneliness
and desolation of the cross as a result of the world's
sin He bore. He was suffering what we should have
suffered eternally. A Negro spiritual about what
took place on Calvary says, "Sometimes it causes

me to tremble, tremble." It should make us tremble to behold what our sin did to our Lord and what it would do to us were it not for His great sacrifice there.

"Why?" is the poignant cry of our Lord from the cross. This word of Christ on the cross is a mystery too sacred and profound for human comprehension. But we know it was our sin that caused that awful moment of aloneness. He loved us with such infinite love that He was willing to endure that abandonment. His heavenly Father had to turn His back on Calvary and enshroud it in darkness as His beloved Son became the sin-bearer for mankind.

But in His dark night of the soul, He still lays hold of God: "My God, My God."

This word of the cross, too deep for us to probe and plumb, was not the last word from Calvary. The final word of Calvary was not despair, but triumph.

In our lives we will experience those tides of the spirit. There will be the low ebbs as well as the high tides. But when there is faithfulness, more sure than the tides of the ocean are the unending tides of His love and grace that will overflow our lives.

During World War II, a nameless Jew hiding in Germany scratched out on a basement wall the Star of David and the lines: "I believe in the sun even when it is not shining. I believe in love even when I do not feel it. I believe in God even when He is silent."

"My God, My God, why have You forsaken Me?" Because Christ uttered those words of despair, we need never utter them. Robert Browning has expressed it memorably:

Yea, once Emmanuel's orphan cry
His universe has shaken,
It went up single, echoless,
"My God, I am forsaken."
It went up from holy lips
Amid His lost creation,
That of those lost,
No son should use
Those words of desolation.

—❦—

Lord of Calvary, the barriers of my sin and pride are broken by Your sacrifice and suffering for me.

38

The Word
of Suffering

*After this, Jesus, knowing that all things
were now accomplished . . . said, "I thirst!"*
—John 19:28

"After this." Our Lord thought of His own need
only after He had made provision for His mother
and by His sacrifice brought redemption for man's
sin and salvation. It was only after Christ had done
all He could for others that He expressed His own
desperate need.

"I thirst." Strange words coming from the lips
of the One who said, "Whoever drinks the water
I give him will never thirst." Strange words coming
from the One who made the oceans and every
river that flows through the valleys and every
stream that cascades in the mountains! Strange
words from the One who made the refreshing rains
and life-giving moisture and the treasures of the
snow!

In His terrible suffering as His throat became
parched and His body seemed on fire as He longed
for a sip of cold water, did He perhaps remember
the cool waters of Galilee? Or the clear cold water

from the well by the woman of Samaria? Or the waves that gently lapped the shore as He strode by the lakeside? Or the dewy grass He so often had felt cooling His sandaled feet?

Unrelieved thirst is one of the greatest physical sufferings humans endure. This word from the cross expresses the excruciating physical agony Jesus suffered on Calvary.

Today Christ still thirsts. He thirsts for our love and devotion. He thirsts for the service He would have us render to His kingdom. He thirsts for our lives to be pure and holy that we may be a reflection of His grace and glory.

For what in life do we thirst? What are the deepest yearnings of our souls? Our desires determine our destiny. May we with the psalmist say, "As the deer pants for the water brooks, So pants my soul for You, O God. My soul thirsts for God, for the living God" (Ps. 42:1–2). Then we shall know the healing waters that flow from Calvary, so beautifully expressed in Albert Orsborn's song:

When shall I come unto the healing waters?
    Lifting my heart, I cry to thee my prayer.
Spirit of Peace, my Comforter and Healer,
    In whom my springs are found,
Let my soul meet thee there.

From a hill I know,
Healing waters flow,

O rise, Immanuel's tide,
And my soul overflow!

Light, life and love are in that healing fountain,
All I require to cleanse me and restore;
Flow through my soul, redeem its desert places,
And make a garden there for the Lord I adore.

—m—

Christ of Calvary, what glories You laid aside and what depth of suffering You endured for me. Such love surpasses my understanding but takes captive my heart.

39
The Word of Atonement

He said, "It is finished!"—John 19:30

Death is the great intruder upon life. It does not wait for us to finish what we are doing. It has a way of coming upon us unaware, in the midst of our work and the business of life. Death is always an interruption. It puts a period in the middle of a sentence in an unfinished book.

There has only been one exception to that rule. Only One who made death wait until His work was done. Only One who could say before He died, "It is finished."

To what was Jesus referring by this word from the cross? A prostitute at Simon's banquet had found forgiveness, but how many more walked the streets? For every ten withered muscles that had been flexed into health, a hundred remained impotent. For the hundreds Jesus had healed, thousands more were ill. It is obvious He was not referring to His healing ministry as having accomplished all that could be done.

Nor did He say, "It is finished," in the manner one would speak of achieving some great feat, or a masterpiece of satisfaction.

At the foot of Mount McKinley in the far north a skeleton seated at the base of a tree was found. Just above were carved these words: "The end of the trail." They told the tragic story of one who had set out to climb that mountain: his strength failed, and he died with his mission unfulfilled. It was not in this sense that Jesus said, "It is finished." He did not mean that He had gone His limit and could go no further. This is not an expression of failure, but an expression of fulfillment.

We can only understand this word from the cross in the context of the atoning work of Christ. At Adam's fall, sin entered into the bloodstream of humanity. Mankind inherited the curse of original sin. This rebellion and transgression against God's moral law of the universe had upon it the penalty of eternal death. There was only one way out.

The highest price had to be paid for the forgiveness of sin and the restoration of fellowship between God and man. Through the centuries the offering of the lamb according to the strict sacrificial rules was just a shadow of the perfect offering of the Lamb of God. On the cross Jesus gave Himself as the perfect offering for the atonement of man's sin. When He said, "It is finished," He meant the scarlet payment had been made for the demands of God's justice. This word speaks to us of the seriousness of sin, the justice of God, and His unspeakable mercy and love.

John R. W. Stott, in *The Cross of Christ*, writes that the cross enforces three truths about ourselves, about God, and about Jesus Christ. "First, our sin must be extremely horrible. Nothing reveals the gravity of sin like the cross. Second, God's love must be wonderful beyond comprehension. Third, Christ's salvation must be a free gift." When Christ cried out, "It is finished," it was the divine declaration that God's wonderful love was giving to man the gift of salvation from the power and penalty of sin. It was the great Emancipation Proclamation for the world!

—⟋⟍—

Crucified Christ, thank You that Calvary included me, my sin, and my salvation.

40
The Word
of Victory

"Father, 'into Your hands I commit My spirit.'"
—*Luke 23:46*

Luke tells us that this word from the cross was spoken "with a loud voice." It was not as though in a final weak effort He managed to mumble these words. Jesus was the Master of death, the Conqueror of the grave. He was not death's victim, but its Victor.

This word of victory by Christ makes it possible for us to share in His triumph over death. Paul exulted in this glorious truth when he recalled the words of an earlier writer: "'O Death, where is your sting? O Hades, where is your victory?' The sting of death is sin, and the strength of sin is the law." But thanks be to God, who gives us the victory through our Lord Jesus Christ" (1 Cor. 15:55–57).

This seventh word from the cross was a quote of Psalm 31:5. Jesus had so saturated His heart and mind with Scripture that it came naturally to Him in the critical hour on the cross.

Jesus had left heaven for thirty-three long years. Now He was going to be reunited with His Father and all the host of heaven. We too can look forward to that great reunion with those of the family of God, some, in the words of Tennyson, "whom we have loved and long since lost awhile."

The surest thing about life is death. May God grant us grace so that when our life has run its course we may be able to pray, "Father, into Your hands I commit my spirit."

We have listened to the seven statements of Jesus from the cross. Never in human history have there been more sacred or sublime words than what our Lord uttered from Calvary. In these moments, eternity invaded time, earth was touched with heaven. If we give these words our serious attention and response, life can never again be the same.

Three of these seven sayings were prayers. He prayed for those who crucified Him. He prayed while He suffered the torments of hell. He prayed while He drew His last breath. Two of His statements were directed to individuals—one to the dying thief and one to His grieving mother and intimate friend. And finally, two of His words declared for all ages what He had come to accomplish.

The New Testament book of Titus summarizes in one forceful verse the threefold purpose of that awful and awesome moment when the Son of God "gave Himself for us" (Titus 2:14). He died for our salvation "that He might redeem us from every lawless deed." He died for our sanctification "that He might . . . purify for Himself His own special people." And He died that we might serve and glorify Him, being a people "zealous for good works."

May we affirm with the poet Elizabeth Clephane:

> Upon that cross of Jesus
> Mine eye at times can see
> The very dying form of One
> Who suffered there for me;
> And from my smitten heart, with tears,
> Two wonders I confess:
> The wonder of His glorious love,
> And my own unworthiness.

—∞—

Jesus, keep me near the cross, that I may remember Your infinite love and mercy and more worthily serve and follow You.

The Triumph of Calvary

*God forbid that I should boast except in the
cross of our Lord Jesus Christ.—Galatians 6:14*

When Lincoln's body was brought by train back
to Springfield, Illinois, a former slave held her
little child up to see the flag-draped casket contain-
ing the great emancipator's body. She said to her
child: "Take a long, long look, honey. That's the
man who died to set us free." As we have contem-
plated the week that brought Christ to Calvary,
we have looked at the One who loved us so much
that He gave His life to set us free. He is the great
Lover and Emancipator of our soul. In the great
phrase of Bonhoeffer, Jesus was "the man for
others."

That humble tree that had grown on a Palestin-
ian hill, used to crucify an outcast of the earth,
felt Jesus' limbs along its common, broken bark.
Today a weary world bows before it to pray. That
cross has become a symbol for the hope of men.
Christ on the cross was not a victim but a Victor.
We commemorate not a tragedy, but a triumph.

The grave and sin retreat before the onward march of Christ the Mighty Conqueror. At Calvary the crucifixion became a coronation.

H. G. Wells was constrained to write, "I am an historian. I am not a believer. But I must confess, as an historian, that penniless preacher from Galilee is irresistibly the center of history." The cross indeed became the hinge of history upon which all else swings.

A little girl, seeing a cross on the communion table in church asked, "Mother, what is that plus sign doing on the Bible?" The cross is God's great plus sign of history. It has balanced the ledger of sinful man with God. It wiped out the spiritual deficit man had against him that had left him spiritually bankrupt before God.

But we must accept God's great gift of salvation through Christ on the cross. The cross only avails for us if we in faith accept Jesus Christ as our Savior. Faith in Christ means believing in Him and turning our lives completely over to His way and will.

The late renowned preacher Robert G. Lee tells that on his first visit to the Holy Land, when he saw the site of Calvary, so great was his excitement that he ran toward it, outdistancing his party. When at last the guide caught up with him, he asked, "Sir, have you been here before?" In a whispered awe, Dr. Lee replied, "Yes, I was here before—nearly two thousand years ago!"

Indeed, we were all at Calvary, nearly two thousand years ago. On the cross the Son of God took our place. By His amazing grace we can be saved and with Him have life abundant in this world and life eternal in the world to come.

I thank God for what Christ did for me on the cross. Because of Calvary, "My name is on the palm of His hand." Those pierced hands of Jesus reached down from that cross and embraced my life in the unspeakable love of the One who hung there. At the age of seventeen, they took hold of the wandering planet of my life and by the force of His mighty love, brought me into the orbit of His purpose and power. And life for me has never been the same since. He gave me His salvation for my sin, His eternity for my time, His power for my weakness, His purpose for all life's future.

And that is the great and glorious message of the cross. The hands that wove the rainbow into a scarf and wrapped it around the shoulders of a dying storm, the hands that created the exquisite geometry of the snowflake and painted the beautiful bell of the lily, the hands that flung the stars and galaxies into space, those hands that were pierced on the cross of Calvary will take hold of our tangled lives and make them whole again!

With Isaac Watts, we are constrained to confess:

When I survey the wondrous cross
   On which the Prince of Glory died,

My richest gain I count but loss,
    And pour contempt on all my pride.

Forbid it, Lord, that I should boast
    Save in the death of Christ, my God;
All the vain things that charm me most,
    I sacrifice them to his blood.

See, from his head, his hands, his feet,
    Sorrow and love flow mingled down;
Did e'er such love and sorrow meet,
    Or thorns compose so rich a crown?

Were the whole realm of nature mine,
    That were a present far too small;
Love so amazing, so divine,
    Demands my soul, my life, my all.

———m———

Triumphant Lord, I pray that through the presence and power of the Holy Spirit, I may ever follow faithfully on the pathway of the cross.

THE AUTHOR

Colonel Henry Gariepy is Editor-in-Chief of The Salvation Army National Publications for the USA with headquarters in Alexandria, Virginia. He is the author of twelve books and many published articles. Two of his books have exceeded 150,000 copies with some going into multiple editions and translations abroad.

The author maintains an active schedule of speaking engagements, including Bible conferences and national writers conferences. He is an outdoor enthusiast and a three-time twenty-six-mile marathon finisher. He earned his Bachelor of Arts and Master of Science degrees at Cleveland State University and was honored by his alma mater with its 1994 Alumni Leadership Award. He and his wife, Marjorie, take great delight in their four children and twelve grandchildren.